INBRED SIN AND

A LIVING SACRIFICE

by
George Asbury McLaughlin

Author of
A Clean Heart

SCHMUL PUBLISHING COMPANY
NICHOLASVILLE, KENTUCKY

Published by Schmul Publishing Co.
PO Box 776
Nicholasville, KY USA

Printed in the United States of America

ISBN 10: 0-88019-594-0
ISBN 13: 978-0-88019-594-2

Visit us on the Internet at www.wesleyanbooks.com, or order direct from the publisher by calling 800-772-6657, or by writing to the above address.

Contents

INBRED SIN

PREFACE

I HAVE NOT BEEN ABLE to find a short, concise work on "Inbred Sin." I find this theme more or less treated in works on kindred subjects. It seems to me there is a demand for such a work, for two or three reasons. 1. Multitudes of otherwise intelligent Christians have little idea of the meaning of the terms "Inbred Sin," "Depravity," etc. 2. There is a soul-cry going up from the best of the justified Church for a better experience. Never was the cry louder or more intense than to-day. 3. We believe this cry is occasioned by the battle waged with self. We believe that a Scriptural understanding of the nature and remedy for inbred sin would be a blessing to many more, as it has been to many who have entered into "the glorious liberty of the sons of God."

If this book should not prove helpful in leading inquiring souls to see their privilege, and throw off "the yoke of inbred sin," we hope, at least, that it may suggest the idea of such a work to some one else who is fully competent to write a book distinctively on this topic.

The truths contained here *have* been helpful to some. May they be helpful to all who desire to know all their privileges in Christ.

—THE AUTHOR

Chapter I
WHAT IS INBRED SIN?

THE TERM "INBRED SIN" is not Scriptural, yet it contains a concise explanation, or comment, on the Scriptural terms, "carnal nature," "our old man," "the flesh," "fleshly lusts," etc. The term "Inbred Sin" expresses the same thing as the theological terms, "total depravity," and "original sin." We believe inbred sin to be the chief cause of backsliding in our churches, and the great cause of the tardy growth of so many, who have been long enough in the way to have become giants in Israel, who yet remain, year after year, in spiritual swaddling clothes. Hence it seems to us proper to present, in concise form, a treatise on this disease of soul, and its cure; especially as we find a widespread ignorance in the matter in the Church of God, among otherwise intelligent Christians.

Inbred sin may be defined, *negatively*, thus: —

1. *It is not sin as an act.* Sin is committed as an *act* in three ways. We speak, or do, or think. Or, in other words, sin as an act is in the word, the deed, or the thought. A person cannot commit actual sin, except in one of these

three directions. The same may be said of sins of omission. Hence all sin, as an act, is either of omission or commission, in thought, word, or deed. But sin in thought, word, and deed, is not inbred sin. Actual sin is the result of inbred sin. Actual sin bears the same relation to inbred sin that the plant bears to its root; the same relation that the eruptions of leprosy (a Scriptural type of sin), bear to the inward disease, — the relation of effect and cause. Inbred sin is a *state* of heart causing outward manifestations of sin. St. James (chapter i. 15), says: "Then when lust hath conceived, it bringeth forth sin." And our Saviour still more forcibly tells us the source of actual sin in Mark vii. 21-23: "For from within, out of the heart of man proceed evil thoughts, adulteries, fornications, murders, thefts, covetousness, wickedness, deceit, lasciviousness, an evil eye, blasphemy, pride, foolishness: all these evil things come from within and defile the man." Outward sin is well catalogued. It is a howling wilderness that produces wild beasts; it is a corrupt heart that produces such sin. The *state* of heart that makes these manifestations is inbred sin.

2. *The appetites of the body are not inbred sin.* Our physical appetites are hunger, thirst, and the sexual. Some have fallen into error here, maintaining that Adam was not created pure and holy, because he possessed physical appetites. Hence, they have considered the body sinful, and have striven to eradicate the appetites, by the punishment of the body, by self-denial, fastings, flagellations, self-tortures, forbidding to marry, seclusion in the cloister and monastery. But sin is in the soul, not in the body. The appetites are an original part of our nature. It is not their use, but their *abuse*, that constitutes sin. God created man in His own image, of "righteousness and true holiness." He gave him a body, with appetites to be regulated and kept only for lawful use. It is for the glory of God to take food sufficient for the wants of the physical man, but excess becomes the sin of gluttony, and so with excess in the other appe-

tites. For "whether we eat or drink, or whatever we do," we are commanded to "do all to the glory of God." Enoch and Abel and others pleased God while in the body. But Scripture says: "They that are in the flesh cannot please God." Hence, "flesh" does not mean the body. Inbred sin, or "flesh," then, does not mean the physical man.

3. *Nor does inbred sin consist in thinking of evil.* A great many good people are much perplexed and hindered at this point. They desire to be right in the sight of God, but thoughts of evil are suggested to their minds, and they think it sin, and are harassed. These thoughts of evil come from two sources: either from the laws of mental association, or by the suggestion of the devil. For instance: A devout soul kneels before God in the spirit of earnest desire. After a few moments of prayer, he finds his mind wandering off onto other subjects, purely by the law of association; a train of thought has been started, and he reproaches himself for wandering thoughts, when his purpose has been pure. His mind has acted naturally, in a manner wholly beyond his control— not sinful at all. Or the subtle enemy of all good injects into the mind suggestions to doubt, or pictures crime or wickedness, so that we cannot help thinking of such things. Herein is the difference between a purified soul and one in whom is inbred sin: A pure heart will spontaneously and instantly feel an abhorrence. Such suggestions will be as repugnant as the touch of a viper. A man who is an un-principled and dangerous villain comes to your house and rings the bell. You come to the door, recognize him, and hear what he has to say. But if you welcome him, invite him in, and are pleased to have such a man in your house, then you become a partner, in a sense, with him in wicked-ness. It did not compromise your character when he knocked at your door, but it did when you took him in so willingly. So when a thought of evil comes to your heart, it does not compromise your character; but if you are glad it came, and welcome it, you were like it in character all the

time. The old adage is so true that we quote it: "We cannot help the unclean birds flying over our heads, but we need not let them build their nests in our hair." *Thoughts of evil are not evil thoughts.* Thoughts of evil become evil thoughts only when they are pleasing to us. Joseph had thoughts of evil suggested to him by the temptress. He could not help thinking about the crime; but he had no desire— it was abhorrent to him. Hence, they were not evil thoughts. A greater than Joseph, when tempted of the devil to make stones into bread in the wilderness, to cast Himself down from a pinnacle of the temple, and to worship the devil, could not refrain from the mental act of thinking of these sins; but He did not dally a moment with the thought; but said: "Get thee behind me, Satan." There was no inbred sin to welcome the suggestion. If we find anything in us that causes sin to appear attractive, we may well cry in fear and trembling: "Create in me a clean heart, O God!"

Inbred sin is that depraved state of the heart which resulted from the loss of original righteousness.

Some in perplexity have asked, "Did God infuse evil properties into the soul?" Certainly not. The "carnal mind" is the result of man's following his own will, having lost the image of God. On the day that Adam sinned he lost the original "righteousness and true holiness" in which he was created. His heart was left to its own devices, and unrestrained by the Divine will (as a voluntary agent), it naturally developed a positive hostility to the will of God. As when life departs from the body, positive corruption begins, so did the soul of Adam on the withdrawal of God manifest that corruption which is called "inbred sin," because it is innate or natural. This is inbred sin: a corrupt state of heart which opposes God and holiness. In the unregenerate this state of heart is not only contrary to the will of God, but must always continue thus, unless God move upon it by His gracious Spirit.

"How helpless Nature lies,
   Unconscious of her load!
The heart unchanged can never rise
   To happiness and God."

This evil nature was transmitted by Adam to his children. It is said (Genesis v. 3): "He begat a son in his own likeness, after his image." This is the statement of the great law of hereditary depravity. His firstborn illustrates this sad truth of original sin, by murdering his brother. This is the state in which we all find ourselves— a tendency of heart away from the Divine will: original sin, which breaks forth into actual transgressions.

To make our subject more practical: How may we detect inbred sin in ourselves? 1. It is that state of heart that makes us *loth* [sic] to do God's will. 2. It is that state of heart that makes us *unwilling* to do the will of God. 3. It is that state of heart that makes it appear easy to do what we know to be wrong, and hard to do what we know to be duty. It was a surprise and a wonderment to the little girl as she felt its risings in her soul, that led her to say: "Mother, why is it that naughty things are always so nice?" It manifests itself in the babe when it has lived but a few weeks, before it has had time to learn evil by example of others. People often speak of "the innocence of the babe," and the expression may well apply as far as actual transgression is concerned. But before the babe knows good from evil, wicked tempers and passions exhibit themselves, which are manifestations of inbred sin. Cases are on record of small children, of a few months in age, becoming so angry as to die in a fit of passion. One of the missionaries states that the Hindoos and Mohammedans almost universally concede the depravity of the race. Among illustrative examples he gives this one from one of the chief men of Lucknow: "The sinfulness of man," said he, "is easy enough understood when we remember that in disposing of a good thing— for instance, milk— we have to carry it to men's doors; and when we wish to furnish that which is evil— that is, sell rum— we have but to open a shop, and they come to us. That is, we will make sacrifices to destroy ourselves, but none to help ourselves." We find ourselves prejudiced against our own convictions of duty and right. Most people find it in what they term their natural disposition. Here is one man, he has a violent temper which he in vain attempts to control. He is off like a flash of powder. Another is naturally sullen and revengeful. Another is inflated with pride, a portion of which he controls, for appearance sake. It is natural for another to be covetous. From his earliest moments he is grasping and seeking his own interests only. Inbred sin is usually what the Apostle speaks of in Hebrews, 12th chapter: "The sin that doth so easily beset you." It fits us as easily as a well-fitted garment. Dr. Watts and Charles Wesley call inbred sin "the seeds of sin," because all outward or actual transgressions spring from it. Charles Wesley calls it "inbred leprosy," likening it to a disease deep-seated in the soul.

"Jesus, a word, a look from Thee
  Can turn my heart and make it clean;
  Purge out the *inbred leprosy*,
  And save me from my *bosom sin.*"

The apostle Paul states it as a law of our being. Now a law is simply a power or method of working. He says in Rom. vii. 21: "I find then a law, that, when I would do good, evil is present with me." And this is the universal consciousness and testimony of the race,— an original disposition, deep-seated in the soul, that contends against our moral sense. It is that in the soul that echoes the voice of Satan, that is so in harmony with him that he asserts a claim to it, and uses it as a vantage ground to capture the man. Jesus said: "Satan cometh, and hath nothing in me." Inbred sin had no place in Him. This is what makes most men an easy prey to temptation. It is this that is the source of all the sorrows and sins of the world. It is this that is the source of all the opposition of this world to godliness. It led men to crucify the Son of God. The Apostle truly says of it: "The carnal mind is enmity against God; for it is not subject to the law of God, neither indeed can be." It will be the chief element of hell, and is hell already begun in the soul while in this life, restrained many times only by surroundings, or Providential interference.

Chapter II
INBRED SIN IS NOT REMOVED BY CONVERSION

THE CONVERSION OF THE SOUL is the most important event in its history. It is the grandest experience in the believer's spiritual life. We do not affirm that it is the greatest experience, *in degree,* but in the sense that the laying of the foundation is of the utmost importance, for it prepares the way for the final laying of the cap-stone. So is conversion the grandest step, because it prepares the way for all others. You cannot take the second step until you take the first. The bridegroom counts it the most fortunate day of his life when he formed acquaintance with his bride, for it made marriage a possibility. Conversion is the great event of experience, for by it the higher degrees of grace are made possible; and by it we become candidates for the second degree, and are put in more favorable conditions for growth in grace. Our relations to God and sin are changed in several particulars. These relations are expressed by the terms "justification," "regeneration," "adoption," etc., denoting changes of relation, which, while not

17

the same in meaning, yet take place at the same time.

Now we find much ignorance as to how much God does at conversion in the Church to-day. We wish, therefore, to show what is accomplished, and what is not accomplished at conversion.

I. What does God do for the Soul in Conversion?

1. *Man, in conversion, became a new creature.* A great many fall into the error in the use of figures of speech, in making them apply in all directions, even to the least details, to particulars that were never intended. We must use an illustration or figure only as far as its author intended. How much did the Holy Spirit intend by the figure of the new birth? We believe the figure was intended to convey the idea that the soul at the new birth became so changed as to have new faculties given it that did not before exist. Before, it had no spiritual perception nor feeling; it was dead to the things of God. Now it, perceives, feels, and wills, in the direction of God's requirements. This is so different from its former condition as to be equal to a new creation, and hence is called "the new birth." Now it sees beauty in God's truth. "The eyes of your understanding being enlightened." Like a man in a clear night, who sees what seems like a large star. A telescope is handed him, and through it he sees that there are two. So the soul now sees old things changed; sees old truths as they are. Once he saw the Gospel truths intellectually, now he sees them spiritually. He also has new affections, so that he loves the things he once hated, and *vice versa*. He has new ambitions. Once he loved to shine for self, and now he loves to shine for God. Now he has longings to see Christ, such as he never had before. Now there is a love to God where there was none before His new faculties prove that a change has taken place in him.

2. *He is acquitted, or pardoned, for all past transgressions.* All sin that he has committed is forgiven. In the

language of the courts of justice, he is justified. Sin, as an act— actual transgression— is forgiven, because he accepts Christ by faith for pardon, having confessed his sins. In the language of Scripture, his sins are "blotted out," "remembered no more against him." He is as free from the claims of the law as if he had never sinned.

3. *He is adopted into the family of God.* "Behold what manner of love the Father hath bestowed upon us, that we should be called the sons of God." He is an heir of God and joint-heir with Jesus Christ. He receives the witness of the Spirit to his adoption. "The Spirit itself beareth witness with our spirit that we are the children of God." As an heir of God, he has a title to heaven, if he continue faithful to God.

4. *This change also gives him power to keep from committing wilful sin.* So low has the standard fallen, that it is currently understood to-day in the Church that a Christian can commit sin, and it will be considered all right if he only asks forgiveness. God is so ready to forgive that we can obey or not, if we only have stated times of asking forgiveness. The Apostle Paul says to those who talked the same way in his day— who seem to think that evening prayer would settle all wilful sin of the day, whether there is an intention to forsake it the next day or not—

"Shall we continue in sin that grace may abound? God forbid. How shall we that are dead to sin live any longer therein?" St. John declares that, "He that is born of God doth not commit sin." He will not intentionally violate one of his Father's commands. *For the term sin, in the New Testament, as an act, always signifies voluntary transgression.* Says Dr. Lyman Abbott, of the Greek verb *hamatano:* "It signifies, in the New Testament, *moral wrong;* never a mere error in judgment." God does not hold us responsible or guilty for sins of ignorance. Paul says: "Where there is no law, there is no transgression"; and again, "Sin is not imputed where there is no law." So that a Christian is one who does not knowingly transgress the commandments of God. So that, by the Divine life in him, he is kept from all those guilty thoughts, words, and acts, of which inbred sin is the root. This is thought by many to be an impossible experience, and absurd doctrine, partaking of the nature of enthusiasm. But it is the enthusiasm of the Bible, nevertheless. It is Scriptural. Said Jesus to the impotent man: "Sin no more, lest a worse thing come upon thee." And the Apostle John, writing to the church, says: "My little children, these things write I unto you, that ye sin not." "Whosoever abideth in him, sinneth not." Says Mr. Wesley, in his sermon on "The First Fruits of the Spirit": "They are not condemned for any present sins, for now transgressing the commandments of God. For they do not transgress them; they do not walk after the flesh, but after the Spirit. This is the continued proof of their 'love of God, that they keep His commandments.'" When a Christian feels within him the stirring of anger, or pride, or envy, or malice, his faith in God is such as to enable him to repress the word, the thought, or the act of sin. If his faith fail not, he may have constant victory, and keep these from outward expression. While some one may say this is not common, average experience, we say it *ought* to be; it is within the possibilities of grace, and is actual, as proved in the experience of some justified Christians. It would be a more general experience, if people had right instructions, as we will attempt to show farther on. The large part of the Church (according to their own testimony of "heart wanderings," "crooked paths," and the like), are in the alternate experiences of backsliding and repentance, which, to say the least, is not favorable to growth. It need not be so, for our God does not wish it to be so, and has made ample provision in the atonement to cover all our need.

5. *Conversion creates abhorrence of inbred sin, and a desire for a pure heart.* It could not be otherwise. Every dutiful child of God loves what his Father in Heaven loves, and hates what his Father in Heaven hates; God loves purity,

and hates impurity; and when a Christian sees sin in himself, he abhors it, for it is contrary to the nature of God whom he loves. For it is impossible to love God and love that which is hostile to God. And sin is contrary to the Divine nature. Conversion is like refreshment to a starving man; it excites all his nature after a fulness of that which he has tasted. It is a spurious conversion that does not beget a thirst after purity of heart and freedom from all inward tendencies to sin. We may well doubt our conversion if we do not desire all the mind of Christ to dwell in us. One writer declares, with a good deal of truth, that "we are guilty of all sin which we do not hate." Every Christian has a hope of seeing Jesus, and of being made like Him. And the Apostle plainly declares: "Every man that hath this hope in him (Jesus) purifieth himself, even as he is pure." One of the strongest evidences that we are converted and not in any degree backslidden, is an intense desire for a pure heart. That is what the true Church of God has been praying all along the ages, in such hymns as, —

> "Oh, for a heart to praise my God!
> A heart from SIN SET FREE,
> A heart that ALWAYS feels Thy blood
> So freely spilt for me."

We do not mean to say that this longing is always so clearly defined, that they know just exactly what they desire. But there is a soul-cry for it that many times has been unable to voice itself. Oh, what responsibility, on the part of preachers and teachers, in leading the flock! We have dwelt on what conversion opens up of experience and privilege because, in these days, if we speak of another degree of grace beyond, a cry is raised that conversion is depreciated. And also for another reason: to help us more clearly to understand what conversion does not do for the soul.

II. *At conversion, all the carnal mind, or inbred sin, is not destroyed*. A very troublesome residuum still remains, which is the chief cause of backsliding, intensifies the power of the temptations of the devil, is the root of the strife we often see among Christians, and is that which demands satisfaction from the world, leading so many followers of God to go to the world for gratification. It is this "inbred corruption" that makes a Christian life so hard to so many; that calls simple duties, that reason would say ought to be considered privileges, heavy crosses. There is but one class of people who have ever denied that the remnants of depravity still remain in the believer. And they cannot be consistent in so doing, as we shall attempt to show in this chapter. They deny it, for what would seem to one not conversant with the matter, to be a singular reason. *They only deny it when a cure is recommended for it.* Like a sick man, to whom a remedy is proposed that he does not wish to take, he will sometimes deny that he is sick in order to escape the remedy. Some people try to make out that they are not sick when they are, hoping thereby to avoid the expense of a physician. They feel as if it were too expensive to have a doctor. But it costs a great deal to be sick, when we might be well. And so they deny that they have any inbred sin— a proposition that is contrary to Scripture, to reason, and to experience, as we shall endeavor to show.

1. *The Scriptures teach that remnants of carnality, or inbred sin, are in the justified believer.* We might cite many instances in the Old Testament. We will, however, mention but one, concerning which, it seems to us, no candid person will entertain any doubt. Inbred sin, in the heart of Jacob, took the form of covetousness. Jacob would have made a good Wall-street broker. But Jacob became a follower of God. At Bethel, he made a covenant to be faithful to God, and God promised that Jacob should be under His especial care and protection. "And Jacob vowed a vow, saying, If God will indeed be with me, and will keep me in this way that I go, and will

give me bread to eat and raiment to put on, so that I come again to my father's house in peace; then the Lord shall be my God" (Gen. xxviii. 20, 21), — a decision and purpose as determined as ever a seeking sinner made to God. And as God had promised to be his God if he made this covenant, we must conclude that he, then and there, became a child of God. And yet we find, again and again, after that, in his dealings with his uncle Laban, that covetousness still lingered in his heart, — his besetting sin.

Let us turn to the New Testament. Paul says to the church at Corinth (1 Cor. iii.): "And I, brethren, could not speak unto you as unto spiritual, but as unto carnal, even as unto babes in Christ. I have fed you with milk, and not with meat: for hitherto ye were not able to bear it, neither yet now are ye able." Here he acknowledges that they were "in Christ," and "brethren," but that they were "carnal," "babes in Christ"; that is, the carnal mind still existed in these brethren. And no one could say to the Apostle, we are pure in heart; we became so when we became brethren; for he tells them in the next verse in what form inbred sin exhibited itself. "For ye are yet carnal: for whereas there is among you envying, and strife, and divisions, are ye not carnal, and walk as men?" This Scripture clearly teaches, then, by the recognition of the Apostle, that we may be "brethren," and yet be "carnal," as evinced in unholy temples. These had not backslidden, for they were "babes in Christ." Neither had inbred sin been destroyed in these "babes in Christ." The Apostle describes, in the seventh chapter of Romans, the struggle of a man with inbred sin. Some have understood in this chapter that a Christian is referred to; others, that it refers only to the unconverted. While it illustrates, in some degree, the case of every one, both saint and sinner, in whom dwells the carnal mind, it seems to us more especially to illustrate the experience of the Christian who has perceived the exceeding spirituality of God's law. It is only a Christian with an abhorrence for sin divinely implanted, who could utter such a heart-rending cry as: "O wretched man that I am! Who shall deliver me from the body of this death?" But the confession of the man is the Scriptural confession of a man in favor with God. Hear him in the twenty-second verse: "For I delight in the law of God after the inward man." Now the man who delights in the law of God, *after the inward man,* is a Christian,— a servant of God. So David says. We take David as authority on this point in the first Psalm. "His delight is in the law of the Lord; and in his law doth he meditate day and night." Of such a man the inspired penman says, "Blessed"; and a little farther on he says: "*The ungodly are not so.*" And yet he may delight in the law of the Lord in the inner man, and yet have the same experience that the Apostle speaks of in the next verse (Rom. vii. 23): "But I see another law in my members, warring against the law of my mind." In the epistle to the Galatians, Paul tells us of this same law of inbred sin in the Galatian Christians, who had "begun in the Spirit," and expected to be "made perfect by the flesh." He says: "This, I say then, walk in the Spirit and ye shall not fulfil the lusts of the flesh. For the flesh lusteth against the Spirit, and the Spirit against the flesh, and these are contrary, the one to the other, so that ye cannot do the things that ye would." Here we have a contest in the hearts of these Galatians between the Spirit and the flesh. Mr. Wesley says on the passage: "But the Holy Spirit, on his part, opposes your evil nature"; and again, in his sermon on "Sin in Believers," he says of the passage: "Nothing can be more express. The Apostle here directly affirms that the flesh, evil nature, opposes the Spirit, even in believers; that even in the regenerate, there are two principles, contrary the one to the other." Inbred sin had come into this church in the same form as at Corinth. The Bible abounds with the teaching that inbred sin exists, in a degree, in the justified. We find, too, that the Thessalonian Church were "in God the Father, and in the Lord Jesus Christ" (1 Thess. i. 1); and yet some things were lacking in their faith (1 Thess. iii. 10). Inbred sin lurked in a state of imperfect faith in the heart that failed to save them from a certain sin that they were as yet ignorant of as displeasing to God.

Chapter III
INBRED SIN NOT REMOVED BY CONVERSION [CONCLUDED]

W E HAVE SHOWN that at conversion the sinner is justified, regenerated, adopted, has the witness of the Spirit, receives a power that will keep him from committing known sin, and feels an abhorrence to everything unholy within or without; that he has a joy and peace such as he never knew before. Let us look at the further experience of the young convert. We have shown that Scripture teaches that there are still remnants of depravity in the heart. We come, then, to see if experience bears us out.

2. *Universal experience confirms this truth.* In the newness of life the young convert goes forth with a bounding heart, feeling "strong in the Lord, and in the power of His might"; ready to do anything for God. He is kept so wonderfully that he never expects to sin again, or have any desire to sin. He hates sin. As the old hymn expresses it:—

"I thought I never should sin any more."

But a sudden temptation comes to him, and he flies into a passion; has lost his temper. What does he do now? A great many get discouraged at this point, doubt their conversion, are led to believe, after all, there is nothing in religion, and give it up. This is the chief reason that there is such a host of people today who had a clear experience of conversion, but for want of instruction at this point have given the whole matter up. This is, we believe, the chief reason why there are so many backsliders. In many communities there are as many as there are professed Christians in the place. *There is a crying-out need of light and instruction on the nature of inbred sin to preserve the fruits of our evangelistic work.* We hear everywhere serious, thoughtful men, lamenting the difficulty in keeping converts in a justified state. We only use this illustration of loss of temper to express one phase of experience; there are other lusts of soul that manifest themselves. Loss of temper is one of the most common. But there are many who are not discouraged from Christian life, even at a break-down like this; they know God has pardoned them, and they are doing as well as they know, and they come and ask God for pardon for the sin committed while in passion, and start on again, resolved next time to be watchful— to lean by faith on Jesus every moment. Again they are tempted, under provocation, to speak the angry word; but, looking to Jesus, crying, "Lord, help!" victory comes. Temper was there, but God gave grace to overcome, and come off without committing actual sin. But the temper *was there.* And if the convert goes on from this time and never yields to it once (a very rare case), yet it is there, and his heart is not pure. How contradictory to all experience is the assertion that Christians are freed from inbred sin at conversion. If such were true, then there have been but a very few conversions, if any, since the world began; for the majority of Christians cannot testify to any such experience. Or, if there have been many conversions, the majority of the Church have been living in a backslidden condition, and are in it to-day; for it is not their experience now. Or the convert may not be afflicted with inbred sin in the form of temper. There are other manifestations. Covetousness lurks in some, and hinders growth in grace. A heart whose tendency is to unbelief; a tendency to backsliding in others; a sullen, sulky, disposition in others; lust tempts others; pride others; love of the world still others; wilfulness still others. At times these have to be struggled against. They are felt at times; we do not say always.* Mr. Wesley says, in his sermon on "The Scriptural Way of Salvation": "Hence may appear the extreme mischievousness of that seemingly innocent opinion, that there is no sin in a believer; that all sin is destroyed root and branch the moment a man is justified. By totally preventing that repentance, it quite blocks up the way to sanctification."

We deem it uncharitable to say that we are saved from inbred sin at conversion, for it would make backsliders of many devoted souls who are serving God to the best of their knowledge, who do feel these lusts of soul. Mr. Wesley says on this point in his sermon on "Sin in Believers" (page 110 Wesley's Sermons): "And as this position— there is no sin in a believer, no carnal mind, no bent to backsliding— is thus contrary to God's Word, so is it to the experience of His children. These continually feel a heart bent to backsliding; a natural tendency to evil; a proneness to depart from God and cleave to the things of the earth. They are daily sensible of sin remaining in their heart, pride, self-will, unbelief; and of sin cleaving to all they speak and do, even their best actions and holiest duties. Yet at the same time they 'know they are of God'; they cannot doubt of it a moment." *So evident is this truth, that all the churches, whether Catholic or Protestant, admit it, in their creeds.* The Council of Trent, whose canons are the highest standards of the doctrines and discipline of the Roman Catholic Church, at its fifth session, held June 17, 1546, issued this confession: "But this holy synod confesses and is sensible, that in the baptized there remains concupiscence, or an incentive (to sin), which, whereas it is left for our exercise, can not injure those who consent not, but resist manfully by the grace of Jesus Christ.

The Greek Church (or Eastern division of the Catholic Church), in the Longer Catechism, speaking on the text, "they that are Christ's have crucified the flesh with the affections and lusts," says: "How can we crucify the flesh with the affections and lusts? By bridling the affections and lusts, and by doing what is contrary to them." The Reformed Church of Germany, in the "Formula of Concord," Art. IV., Sec. 8, says: "But we acknowledge that this liberty of spirit in the elect children of God is not perfect, but is as yet weighed down with manifold infirmity, as St. Paul laments concerning himself about this matter" (Rom. vii. 14-25; Gal. v. 17); and again, Art. VI., Sec. 3: "And they that believe, according to the spirit of their mind, have perpetually to struggle with their flesh; that is, with corrupt nature, which inheres in us even till death. And on account of the old Adam which remains fixed in the intellect and will of man, and in all his powers, there is need that the law of God should always shine before man, that he may not frame anything in matters of religion under an impulse of self-devised devotion, and may not choose out ways of honoring God not instituted by the Word of God."

In the "Helvitic Confession" of the Swiss Churches we find this statement: —

"*Secondly*, in the regenerate there remains infirmity. For since sin dwells in us, and the flesh struggles against the spirit in renewed persons, even unto the end, the regenerate are not able at all readily to accomplish what they undertake. This is confirmed by the Apostle in the Epistle to the Romans, chap. vii., and Gal. v."

The Heidelberg Catechism of the Reformed Church, published in 1563, asks thus:

"*Question* 56. What dost thou believe concerning the *forgiveness of sins?*

"*Answer.* That God, for the sake of Christ's satisfaction, will no more remember my sins, neither the sinful nature with which I have to struggle all my life long; but graciously imparts to me the righteousness of Christ, that I may nevermore come into condemnation."

The Confession of the Church of France, prepared by Calvin, contains in Art. XI.: "Even after baptism it is still of the nature of sin, but the condemnation of it is abolished for the children of God, out of His mere free grace and love; and further, that it is a perversity always producing fruits of malice and rebellion, so that the most holy men, although they resist it, are still stained with many weaknesses and imperfections while they are in this life."

The Belgic Confession of the churches of the Netherlands, Art. XV., says: "Nor is it," (original sin) "by any means abolished, or done away in baptism, since sin always issues from this woful source as water from a fountain; notwithstanding it is not imputed to the children of God unto condemnation, but by His grace and mercy is forgiven them. Not that they shall securely rest in sin, but that a sense of this corruption should make believers often to sigh, desiring to be delivered from the body of this death."

The Church of Scotland, in Art. XIII. of its Confession, says of conversion: " And fra thine cummis that continuall battell, quhilk is betwixt the flesh and the Spirit in God's children."

Art. IX. of Church of England declares: "And this infection of nature doth remain, yea, in them that are regenerate."

Art. XXIV. of the Irish Church is as follows: "This corruption of nature doth remain, even in those that are regenerated, whereby the flesh lusteth against the Spirit, and cannot be subject to the law of God."

Also the third Canon of the Synod of Dart:

"By reason of these remains of indwelling sin, and the temptations of sin and of the world, those who are converted could not persevere in a state of grace, if left to their own strength." The Westminster Confession contains these words: "There remaineth still some remnants of corruption in every part, whence ariseth a continual war, the flesh lusting against the Spirit, and the Spirit against the flesh." This agreement of all the creeds is on a matter of experience. Their lack of experience, deeming it *necessary* to contend against inbred sin all through life, proves nothing. While experience proved that the life of Israel in the Wilderness was unpleasant at times, their ignorance of Canaan did not disprove its existence or its glories. So these creeds do voice an experience of the renewed man struggling against inward evil, establishing the point that inbred sin is in the justified believer; but these creeds do not prove that it must be so until death. Mr. Wesley says in his sermon on "Sin in Believers": "The same testimony is given by all other churches; not only the Greek and Romish Church; but by every reformed church in Europe of whatever denomination"; and again: "It hath been observed before, that the opposite doctrine, that there is no sin in believers, is quite new in the Church of Christ; that it was never heard of for seventeen hundred years, — never until it was discovered by Count Zinzendorf. I do not remember to have seen the least intimation of it, either in any ancient or modern writer; unless, perhaps, in some of the wild, ranting Antinomians." We have shown that Scripture gives no warrant to believe that sin is all destroyed in justified believers, that this is confirmed in the experience of converts, and that this is the universal testimony of all the churches, as voiced in their creeds.

3. *And it is contrary to the reason of the thing.*

(1) It is unreasonable, for it contradicts the universal tes-

timony of all Christendom. For human nature is the same in all ages, and the working of the Gospel is the same.

(2) Inbred sin never was forgiven, and never can be forgiven, either in this world or the world to come. It is not one of those things that forgiveness *could* touch. Forgiveness is granted only for those things that we *do;* not for what we *are* by nature. Inbred sin is not a deed, but a *state.* No physician forgives a *disease.* A child disobeys its parent and enters upon a course that destroys health. A deadly fever is the result. He sends for his father and is forgiven for his acts of disobedience, yet no rational man would say that is all he needs; no sane man would say that you can forgive disease. He needs to be *healed* as well as forgiven. The forgiveness of the father does not cure the sickness. He needs something beyond that— another work that requires a physician. But when it comes to man's soul, the same fact is still more evident. The son contracted his disease, but we *inherit inbred* sin; *we are not responsible for its existence in our souls.* Not being responsible for it, we are not guilty because of it. We are guilty only when we knowingly commit actual transgression.

(3) *A penitent sinner desires pardon for actual sin so much that he rarely, if ever, at all thinks of inbred sin.* His guilt being on account of actual transgression, he hastes to get rid of the condemnation, by applying for immediate pardon. That is all he thinks of at that time. He is like the ancient fugitive escaping to the City of Refuge. He has no time to think about the state of his health; he is anxious to get into the city ere the manslayer cuts him down. So an unconverted man, convicted, sees only his sins that condemn him. Inbred sin does not condemn him. Justice will cut him down for his actual transgressions, and so his only plea is for forgiveness for actual transgression. No one ever thinks, in praying for him, to do more than to pray that his sins may be forgiven, and his heart regenerated, and the witness of the Spirit given him.

(4) *So absurd is the idea that inbred sin is removed at conversion that those who maintain this heresy never testify definitely to the fact.* It is customary for those who say God has done a complete work for them in conversion, if asked if all evil tempers and desires have been removed from their hearts, to hesitate and stammer and equivocate. While, if you ask the same persons if they have been converted, they reply, "Yes," without a moment's hesitation. In the latter case, they have the witness of the Spirit to the fact of their acceptance with God. In the former they have not the witness of the Spirit; God does not uphold them in their testimony, and hence they cannot give an unhesitating answer. They break down. Mr. Wesley said that while there might be persons who had received such a work of grace at their conversion, he had never heard of one. If there be any such well-authenticated cases, they are remarkable examples, such as are not met every day, and our leaders in Israel ought to turn their attention to such exceptional instances that were never known in the Church for centuries, and examine and get at the secret of this wonderful phenomenal experience.

(5) *The absurdity of this is seen in the fact that no one ever instructs penitent sinners to ask for the removal of inbred sin at conversion.* A convert gets just as far as his faith takes him. He is told that by trusting Jesus, his sins are forgiven. He believes on the testimony of others, and of the Word of God. He could not believe for the forgiveness of sins unless he had some instruction on that point. "Faith cometh by hearing." If he had never heard that God is willing to pardon sin, he would not have applied. And the reason that sinners do not have the roots of sin all extracted at conversion, is, they have never felt the need of it, have never been instructed as to its necessity, nor that God wants to do it at that time; hence do not believe for it; and as salvation comes only by faith, not having believed, they do not receive what they do not expect.

We may, before closing this chapter, stop to notice the objection usually raised at this point. It is often said: "I gave my all to God at conversion, and He did the whole work for me then. When God does a work, He does a perfect work. He does not do any half-way work." This sounds very plausible and very reasonable, but it is an unfair statement. It assumes that other people accuse the Lord of performing only a half-way work, which is not the case. God does perform a perfect work at conversion. He *perfectly converts*. And we can find no passage where He promises more than that at conversion. But perfect conversion is not perfect cleansing. He must be converted to see the spirituality of God's law. *That* he cannot see in his sins. For he is "dead in trespasses and sins." He must have new faculties, in order to see the spirituality of God's laws. He is converted in order to put him where he may intelligently see the loathsome corruption of inbred sin. To those who say God always does it all the first time he touches, we would point to the healing of the blind man, who at the first touch saw men as trees walking; at the second touch he saw clearly. Christ did not do the whole work of healing in his case first, but worked perfectly as far as He wished to go in the first work. And He touches the soul in conversion, in order to prepare it for something more. The record teaches that He did not create all things in one day. But He made each day's work perfect in itself, and a preparation for the next day. Would it not be better to consult Scripture, the experience of the ages and reason, than to assert such theories that cannot be sustained?

(6) *People who assert that there is no inbred sin in believers cannot be consistent.* We give an illustration of a single denomination. When converts had come in the past complaining of inbred sin, they had said, You must endure that all your life. When the contrary began to be preached, and a way of deliverance was pointed out, we are told that the same leaders who had preached "You must endure it," now

turned round and said, "you were delivered from it all at conversion." They had rather deny the sickness, then take the medicine.

Chapter IV
INBRED SIN REMOVED BEFORE WE ENTER HEAVEN

IT IS HARDLY NECESSARY to dwell at length on this topic. We are writing to those who do not accept the sensual heaven of the Mohammedans, nor the gross heaven of Paganism, but who believe in the heaven of the Bible; the home of the pure and holy; to those who believe in a God who is holy; who invites men to become His children, in order that they may dwell with Him forever. Hence:—

1. *From the very nature of the case, inbred sin must be destroyed in order to live with Him.* To suppose it possible to dwell a moment in His presence, with His angelic hosts and the spirits of just men made perfect, with any sin in us, is an idea too incongruous to be mentioned. These angelic hosts, we are told, cry, "Holy, holy, holy, is the Lord of Hosts!" Now "how can two walk together except they be agreed?" No soul can live in perfect accord with a holy God who has the least of sin in him; for God cannot look upon sin with the least degree of allowance. He can never be pleased with it, and if He should admit it into Heaven in any form, it would destroy the very idea of Heaven,

which is the abode of the pure and the holy. It would be a surrender of the Divine aversion to sin.

2. *We know this from the teachings of Scripture.* The Revelation declares of the Heavenly City: "And there shall in no wise enter into it anything that defileth, neither whatsoever worketh abomination or maketh a lie" (Rev. xxi. 27). The Apostle declares: "Without holiness no man shall see the Lord." David asks, "Who shall ascend into the hill of the Lord, or who shall stand in His holy place? He that hath clean hands and a pure heart; who hath not lifted up his soul to vanity, nor sworn deceitfully." From the nature of the case, and from the express teachings of Scripture, we know that inbred sin must be removed before we enter Heaven.

Chapter V
INBRED SIN DESTROYED— WHEN? WHERE?

BEFORE WE ENTER HEAVEN. All intelligent Christians admit it. How soon before?

1. *Not in any future purgatory*. The Roman Catholic Church has invented the dogma of purgatory as the only consistent way out of a dilemma. It refuses to believe that indwelling sin can be removed in this world, and so has recourse to future fires of purification, to prepare us for Heaven. Akin to this is the teaching of Restorationism. The Roman Catholic Church is more consistent than many Protestants. We, as Protestants and evangelical Christians, deny purgatory as contrary to the Scriptures, and as detracting from the doctrine of the atonement of Christ. We believe that the Scriptures teach that "departed souls go immediately, at death, to a fixed state of happiness or misery." "Blessed are the dead that die in the Lord from henceforth" (Rev. xiv. 13). "He that is unjust, let him be unjust still; and he which is filthy, let him be filthy still; and he that is righteous, let him be righteous still; and he that is holy,

let him be holy still" (Rev. xxii. 13). As believers in the Word of God, we have found that it must be removed ere we enter Heaven.

2. *Inbred sin not destroyed by death.* We do not believe in purgatory; we are forced, then, to one of two things. *Inbred sin is removed while we are dying, or before we die.* Let us look at the first thought. Is it removed while we are dying? Surely no one has a right to say it is at that time, unless he has good reason for it, founded on Scripture or experience. What we *think* in the matter does not help the case. One thing is certain, there is no good reason to suppose that it is removed by death, unless there be something intrinsically powerful in death. Death contains nothing in itself antagonistic to sin. In fact, death is the *result* of sin. The result cannot destroy the cause. Death is privative; that is, it is simply the absence of life. To make death the destruction of sin, is to be like the ancient heathen who believed sin was in matter, and not in the soul, which is absurd, and would destroy all human responsibility. The separation of soul and body (which is all there is of death), will not purify the soul; there is nothing in any way connected with death that destroys sin, and no candid man will assert it unless he has some proof to offer. "Death came by sin"; but sin's destruction does not come by death. Death is said, in the Scriptures, to be our enemy; but if death should destroy sin, it would be one of our best friends. But "the last enemy that shall be destroyed is death." Our other enemies will, then, all be destroyed before the resurrection morn. Sin will be destroyed therefore, before that time. If it is certain that inbred sin is destroyed in the hour and article of death, yet even then it is not death that does it. Almighty power must do it even then; and if God is able to do it then, He is able to do it before that time. Does Christ have to employ death as an assistant in the destruction of sin? Can He do it only when He can get us where the world and sin can no longer tempt us? What absurd notions these

are! Some doctors can put an end to disease only by kill-
ing the patient; but the Great Physician can kill the disease of sin, and allow the patient to live in this world in
better health than ever. And if He cannot do it directly by
a stroke of Almighty power, then no one can, for —

3. *Inbred sin cannot be removed by human power.* All
schemes that promise to remove it by culture, are a failure.
People have said educate, culture, polish, and men thus
developed will see the heinousness of sin and shun it. But
there are no converts of this theory who confess it is done.
The most highly educated will lose his temper as easily as
one who is not. The most refined will feel as angry inside
as any other, even if he represses it. To educate and polish
a bad heart will not take out pride, but usually inflates it
the more. Polish a black heart, and it is simply a black
heart polished. It is in vain to say I will not henceforth feel
ugly, or be covetous. It is *there* just the same, after all effort. How many times men have said, in their hearts, "It is
wrong for me to feel as I do, and I will try to get above it."
Yes, but it is there, even if you get above it; if you do not
give way to it. Preventing dynamite from exploding does
not remove it. Something else must be done. All theories of
culture or naturalism only discredit Jesus, the Sin-destroyer,
and pronounce His mission a failure.

4. *Almighty Power is the only remedy that will destroy
inbred sin.* The Maker of the heart created it pure; His work
has been impaired by an enemy, and only the Almighty
can put the heart right and keep it so. He who created the
heart "in righteousness and true holiness," alone can re-
store it. The Scripture is very plain on this point; so plain
that skeptics and opposers admit that is the teaching of
the Bible. The prophet Zechariah says of this dispensation:
"In that day there shall be a fountain opened to the house
of David" (to the Church), "for sin and for uncleanness,"
both the outward and inward (chap. xiii. 1). "He shall re-
deem Israel from all his iniquities." From *all; i.e.,* inward

and outward (Psalm cxxx. 8). "Bless the Lord, O my soul, and forget not all His benefits, who forgiveth all thine iniquities, who healeth all thy diseases" (Ps. ciii. 3). Here actual and inbred sin are taken away. "Speak ye comfortably to Zion" (the marginal is, "Speak ye to the heart of Zion" — nothing would comfort the heart of Zion more in these days than to know that inbred sin may be destroyed), "and cry unto her that her warfare is accomplished; that her iniquity is pardoned; for she hath received of the Lord's hands *double* for all her sins" (Isaiah xl 2). Sin is double, — inward and outward, actual, original, — so we need to receive double to get rid of it all. That is just what the Church have been singing all these years: —

"Be of sin the *double* cure,
  Save from wrath and make me pure."

The second line explains the word "double" in the first line. We propose to take our salvation "double"; and this book is written to persuade others to accept the "double cure." When the leper was cleansed the priest took of the blood of the trespass offering and put it on the tip of his right ear, and upon the thumb of his right hand, and the toe of his right foot, thus typifying the blood of Jesus as shed for the justification of the sinner; then "the second time" he took oil and placed it on the blood-stains on the ear, thumb, and toe. It was *oil upon the blood*. Oil was used in healing disease among the ancients, and oil is a type of the Holy Spirit; thus was the entire cleansing of the sinner, *after* his pardon by the Spirit, typified (Lev. xiv.). "Thou shalt call His name Jesus, for He shall save His people *from* their sins" (Matt. i. 21).

John speaks of two baptisms; one with water for the remission of sins, the other "with the Holy Ghost and with fire." He explains in the next verse that it is to be for purification. Fire purifies, removes dross. Jesus said, "I am the vine, ye are the branches": that is, every one who becomes a branch, becomes so by conversion. Then He says: "Every branch in me that beareth fruit He purgeth (purifieth) that it may bring forth more fruit" (John xv.). Here, then, we see that we are first made Christians (branches), and then cleansed, in order that all sour sap may be removed, that we may the better bear fruit. In John xiii. Christ said to the disciples: "He that is washed, needeth not, save to wash his feet, but is clean every whit." They were clean, all but their feet. If their feet had been clean, they would have been clean every whit. Dr. Adam Clark says it is certain they took a bath before this supper (see his note on John xvii. 1). Now they needed to have the remaining defilement of the feet cleansed away. Here are two washings, one of regeneration, the other of the feet (typifying the extremities of our being). Washing was always symbolic of heart cleansing among the Jews. Dr. Lyman Abbott says, on this passage, in his notes on the New Testament: "It treats of the double cleansing wrought by Christ,— the washing of the whole nature in regeneration, and the cleansing of specific sins in sanctification." If we confess our sins, He is faithful and just to forgive us our sins, and to cleanse us from all unrighteousness" (1 John i. 9). If we neutralize the last part of this promise, we must the first. We must treat it just as emphatically and definitely as the first. If we say it is visionary, so is the promise of pardon. If we say it cannot be, so must we say of pardon in first part of verse. If we say it is gradually done, so must we say of pardon, in first part. If we say we can never be certain of it, so must we of the first part of the promise. If we say we cannot be cleansed from all unrighteousness in this life, we vitiate the first part, that says we may be pardoned. This passage is a hard one to those who limit this power of God. Let us beware how we bring Scripture *down to our opinions*. But are there any instances in Scripture that show this? Yes; their number is legion. Gen. xv. tells us the time when Abraham was justified by faith. Two chapters on,

God said: "Walk thou before me, and be thou perfect." Abraham proposed to obey, and we see a change in his nature right there, all hindrances to his serving God with a perfect heart were removed; for we see that his name was changed. Names always stood for character in the Old Testament. *And a change of name meant a change of character.* His character was farther changed, although justified, in the fifteenth chapter.

Jacob became the Lord's at Bethel, as the account plainly indicates; for he and the Lord made a covenant. Inbred sin remained in his heart in the form of covetousness. At Peniel he commenced to pray to be delivered from Esau; but like many a soul to-day, while in prayer God gave him a view of self, and he forgets Esau, and prays for himself. "I will not let thee go except thou bless *me*." He is blessed, and his name and character changed by the Almighty One. Speaking of it in Gen. xlviii. 16, he tells us that he was redeemed from *all evil* at that time. So Isaiah, the prophet, had his lips touched with a coal from the Holy Altar, and the seraph who laid it on his mouth said: "Thine iniquity is taken away, and thy sin is purged." He had all the hindrances to his preaching the Gospel taken away (Isaiah vi.).

David so believed in being saved from inbred sin, which took the form of lust in his soul, and caused him to commit adultery, that after praying for forgiveness of inbred sin, he cries: "Behold, I was shapen in iniquity, and in sin did my mother conceive me." "Purge me with hyssop, and I shall be clean; wash me, and I shall be whiter than snow." And again: "Create in me a clean heart, O God." David's theology was sound. He did not pray for an impossibility; but he was cured of his bosom sin. The baptism of the Holy Ghost, at Pentecost, destroyed the fickleness tending to backsliding, envies and jealousies, of the disciples. Their names had been written in heaven before this (Luke x. 20). They had cast out devils and preached the Gospel by Divine commission. Christ had said that they were not of the world (John xvii. 16); and yet they needed inbred sin wholly destroyed. Peter tells us what they got at Pentecost in Acts xv. 9, while explaining another point,— that their hearts were purified by faith. At the great revival at Samaria, under Philip (Acts viii.), although many were converted and baptized, yet the disciples came down, and God imparted to these converts the Holy Ghost to purify their hearts, just as He did to the disciples at Pentecost.

Cornelius was "a devout man, one that feared God, with all his house, which gave much alms to the people, and prayed to God alway "— a man of whom Peter said, he was accepted of God: "Of a truth I perceive that God is no respecter of persons; but in every nation he that feareth God and worketh righteousness is accepted of Him." Cornelius would, in this day, be invited to join any of our churches, and be considered a pillar of the Church. *We wish the whole Church were up to Cornelius' experience before Peter came to him*. But he still needed the Holy Ghost. Under Peter's preaching, he received the Holy Ghost; and the last remains of inbred sin were purified away. (See Acts xv. 9, which shows that he got just what the disciples did at Pentecost.) The Church at Corinth were brethren, yet carnal (1 Cor. iii. 1). Inbred sin took in them the form of envy and jealousy, the source of all their troubles. They needed it removed. Paul had preached to them, and grace had converted them. He writes: "And in this confidence I was minded to come unto you before that ye might receive a second benefit." *Grace* is the marginal reading (2 Cor. i. 15). And in the seventh chapter, first verse, he urges them to cleanse themselves from "*all* filthiness of the flesh and spirit." In the twelfth of Hebrews, Paul, talking to "brethren"— not unconverted men— says: "Lay aside every weight, and the sin that doth so easily beset you." The figure is of a runner in a race, throwing off his garment that hindered him. The sin that just fits us, as closely as a well-fitting garment, is to be thrown aside. Inbred sin fits just that way. Paul prays for the Thessalonian Church, of which he says in chap. v. 1, "which is in God the Father, and in the Lord Jesus Christ," which had not backslidden, and yet had a lack in their faith, as he says in chap. iii. 10: "Night and day praying exceedingly that we might see your face, and perfect that which is lacking in your faith." They seemed to be troubled with doubts; inbred sin caused a weakness of faith, and they needed inward lust removed. He prayed that this *best Church that he ever founded* might be sanctified wholly (1 Thess. v. 23): that is, cleansed from inbred sin and filled with the Holy Spirit, (That is the meaning of entire sanctification.) We see, then, from these passages of Scripture that there is a work of grace, after conversion, definite and explicit. The hymnology of the Church, which is experience, teaches the same thing. Charles Wesley sings, hymn 486, "Methodist Hymnal ": —

"Speak the SECOND time, be clean.
   Take away my inbred sin."

And again, hymn 491, "Methodist Hymnal":

"Let us all in Thee inherit,
   Let us find that SECOND rest;
   Take away my bent to sinning."

In the volume of hymns published by the Wesleys in 1749, is this stanza:

"Unfold the hidden mystery,
   The SECOND gift impart;
   Reveal Thy glorious self in me,
   In every waiting heart." (p. 195.)

Not to save us from our inbred sin is a reflection on either the ability or the willingness of the Lord. We are not of the number who dare "limit the Holy One of Israel." Let those who will, take the responsibility of denying that the power that created a universe, and upholds it, cannot keep a human soul clean. The objector says: "I believe He is able, but not willing." That is, then, a reflection on His character. If He is able to cleanse us from the sin which we hate, and which *He* hates more than we, and yet we say He is unwilling, we reflect on His character of holiness and mercy. We the same as say, He is pleased to have us go on, defiled by sin. We make a holy God pleased to have His children unholy, when we read that He has given unto us "exceeding great and precious promises" that "we" might be partakers of the Divine nature, *"having escaped the corruption that is in the world through lust."* No. God is not pleased to have any of the works of the devil in His children. God is pleased with the plan of salvation. But He could not be pleased with a plan that did not liberate from all sin; for, to be pleased with such a plan, would be to be pleased with sin, which is impossible and absurd. We have simply quoted a list of passages proving two operations or works of grace. We have not time to quote farther the passages that treat of the entire extinction of sin in this life; their number is legion, all through the Word of God. They may be summed up in one idea. Jesus, the perfect Physician, whose remedy is adequate to every disease of the soul, *at the very time of the sickness or disease.*

5. *God destroys inbred sin instantaneously.* We have already shown that the Bible and experience go to show that it is not destroyed wholly at conversion. We have shown that we cannot enter heaven with such a state of heart. It must be renewed, then, while we are alive. Some go as far as this with us, but stop here, and try to believe that God does this gradually. But there are two remarkable facts that cannot be satisfactorily gainsaid:—

1. *There is no Scripture that teaches that Christ gradually destroys sin.*

2. *There are no witnesses to this theory.* People who have taught, and tried to believe the gradual theory, find that, after years of struggle with temper, it is just as

quick as ever. We never yet heard or read of one who testified that Jesus, after so many years of waiting and praying and believing, has gradually cleansed their hearts from all sin. But we do hear of thousands who declare it was done in an instant. And why not? Has not God the power to do it instantly? Who will say He is unwilling? And as we look still farther and see that it is done by faith — that all the salvation we ever get is by faith, — that our salvation is according to our faith, — and when we remember that faith is an *instantaneous process,* salvation that comes through faith is also instantaneous. When our faith comes to the instantaneous point, then comes salvation. Salvation never comes at any other time. It is impossible to gradually believe, so that we doubt less to-day, and believe more than yesterday.

Here is Mr. A, of whom we say: "I have some doubts about his integrity." In other words, we do not quite believe him. And we never can be said to believe in him unless we cast away all our unbelief. We can never be said to trust God for salvation until we throw away all our unbelief.

While we doubt *at all,* we do not believe; it is only by unmixed faith that we are saved: "Whatsoever is not of faith is sin." Mr. Wesley says on the point of instantaneous faith: "What is *time* necessary for? It must be either to do or suffer. Whereas, if nothing be required but simple faith, a moment is as good as an age."

The Scripture gives us no warrant for purification of sin save by faith. *"Purifying their hearts by faith"* (Acts xv. 9), "sanctified by faith" (Acts xxvi. 18). Says Mr. Wesley, in his sermon on "The Scriptural Way of Salvation": "If you seek it by faith, you may expect it *as you are;* and if as you are, then expect it *now.* It is of importance to observe that there is an inseparable connection between these three points: expect it *by faith;* expect it *as you are;* and expect it *now."* If God can destroy it at death, He can an hour before death; and if an hour, then a year as well.

6. *Growth in grace will never destroy sin.* There are many who do not enjoy the Scriptural theory of faith. They say when it is mentioned: "We believe in growth in grace." As if God intended to destroy inbred sin in that way. Growth in grace is all right in its place, but it is not in growth to destroy sin. The growing apple on the bough will never outgrow any speck of rot in it. Both will grow together until harvest if there is health enough in the apple to endure it; if not, it will all turn to rot. A patient with a cancer needs something besides development; he needs the poison removed from his system. There is much misapprehension as to what growth in grace is. Many, who say they believe in growth in grace, cannot give us a Scriptural definition of grace. They seem to look upon it as an outside agency, neither human nor Divine, that is unconsciously at work in the heart. Others seem to think it means human doing or faithfulness that will gradually wear away sin, as falling water wears away the rock. Grace means "favor." In Scripture, wherever we find the word grace, the sense will be the same if we substitute "favor," — the favor God bestows on us. Jesus "grew in favor with God" (Luke ii. 52),— same Greek term *(karis)* that is, in other passages, translated "grace." Christ grew in "grace" (favor with God), but it had nothing to do with outgrowing inbred sin, for He had no inbred sin to outgrow. And that is what we are to do to grow in favor with God, and in the knowledge of God; but it does not refer to outgrowing sin. But some will start back and say, Christ had no inbred sin, and it is sacrilegious to compare His experience with ours. Not so. We are to grow in favor with God as He did, after we are freed from inbred sin. We grow tardily before that. The same things are said of the believer's experience and of Christ's experience all through the New Testament. They are both born of the Spirit; both baptized of the Holy Ghost; both

crucified, the one for sin, the other to sin (see Romans vi.); both are resurrected from their death of crucifixion. "If ye, then, be risen with Christ, seek those things which are above" (Col. iii.1). We are told to "let this mind be in you which was also in Christ Jesus." Hence it is not presumption to say the growth in grace is the same in *kind,* in Christ and all His brethren. It was growth of His *human* nature. Says Adam Clarke on this passage: "From this we learn that if a man were as pure and perfect as the man Jesus Christ Himself was, yet He might, nevertheless, increase in the image and consequently in the favor of God. So the point is established by Scripture that growth in grace may take place where there is no sin; that growth in grace does not mean growing less and less sinful each day. For it was not so in Christ. No man can be in favor with God who does not believe His Word. For, "Without faith it is impossible to please God." We cannot retain favor or grace with God if, when we read such promises as, "purifying their hearts by faith," we then refuse to believe that our hearts may be purified by faith, and expect it by some kind of a growth. Growth is a development of holy forces in the soul, not a conflict between holy and unholy forces. The latter would be conquest, not growth. If we expect to grow in favor with God, we must not limit His power by denying His great promises. There is neither a gradual pardon nor a gradual cleansing mentioned in the Word of God. As we advance in Christian experience, God shows us new experiences, as within the possibilities of Christian life. We are to enter on them as fast as we are ready for them. He convicts us of our needs and opens our spiritual eyesight; and we receive, by faith, these experiences, so that we go on "from grace to grace." The Apostle seems to have this in mind when he writes to the Romans (v. 1): "Therefore, being justified by faith, we have peace with God, through our Lord Jesus Christ." Here God shows us the grace, "favor" of justification, which we enter by faith. If we are true to the light of this grace, He shows us another grace after justification. "By whom, also, we have access, by faith, into this grace wherein we stand, and rejoice in hope of the glory of God" (verse 2). Here the favor of God is shown as a state where we may stand and rejoice; the hindrance to our standing being removed (inbred sin is the hindrance), the standing grace of a clean heart is the grace spoken of here, where we shall be more likely to stand firm and joyous. This state we see by the text is entered by faith; and so the way to "grow in grace" is to *get into* each grace, first by faith, then keep believing God, and we shall keep growing in favor with Him just as a son who loves and trusts and obeys his father grows in favor or grace with him. *For the moment we stop trusting God for more of His salvation, we are not growing in grace.* This being true, growing in grace is trusting God for deeper, richer experience as fast as He gives us light on privilege, receiving it by faith, trusting Him to destroy the sin as soon as He shows us our privilege. Why do not more people grow constantly in the Divine favor? Because inbred sin so tempts them to disbelieve God that they often disobey Him,— believe for a little time, then doubt and lose the favor of God,— then cry for forgiveness, and get favor again. Thus they lose many higher experiences, because they have to go over the same ground as they did to get converted. But the man who constantly believes, constantly grows in favor. The Bible says: "According to thy *faith* be it unto thee," not according to thy development.

Chapter VI
THE PRESENT DESTRUCTION OF INBRED SIN A GREAT ADVANTAGE

1. G*OD WANTS HOLY PEOPLE on earth.* It has doubtless occurred to the thoughtful reader to ask the question: What has become of those who have died so triumphantly in the faith of Christ, who never knew it was their privilege to be freed from inbred sin? We reply that every honest soul, living up to all the light he has, will be saved. If he is a heathen in Africa, rejecting no light, living as well as he knows how, he will be saved. If he be a Christian, living up to a greater light, he will be saved. No man is responsible for any more light than he has; but all have some light, and are responsible for that. "This is the light that lighteth every man that cometh into the world." Paul tells us how all are judged. "For as many as have sinned without law, shall be judged without law; and as many as have sinned in the law, shall be judged by the law" (Rom. ii. 12). They who have been true to their light will be saved. If they have not heard of their privilege to be cleansed from inbred sin, they did not reject it. If they had seen

their privilege, felt it a duty, and then refused, they would have gone into condemnation, and lost their standing with God. We believe that the wonderful experiences of the death-bed of God's saints who never understood it to be their privilege to be cleansed from inbred sin, are experiences in purification of heart, to make them "meet to be partakers of the inheritance of the saints in light." God purified their hearts in the dying hour. *But God wants holy people on this earth as well as in heaven.* He wants His children to reflect Him here. "Let your light so shine that men may see your good works, and glorify your father which is in heaven." We cannot reflect Him unless we are holy. And He therefore says: "Be ye holy": a command that can no more be modified or weakened, or made to refer to the next world, than, "Thou shalt not steal," or the command to repentance.

2. *This experience is religion made easy.* Candid people have asked the question: "Why do I need it? I commit no wilful sin now." Thank God for that. We wish the whole Church were living in that experience. But even if we are not consciously breaking any of God's commands, we find it difficult, at times, to keep some of them; for instance, to love our enemies, because of tendencies or tempers that rise in our souls. If they were not there, it would be easier doing God's will, and we should not be in so much danger of backsliding and final apostasy. If the enemy inside were cast out, we should have more time to wage aggressive warfare against the devil. We may be able to contend against tramps, but it takes too much time and strength; better send for the police. When inbred sin troubles, send for the Sin-destroyer, Jesus. We are called to a nobler warfare than to be simply holding the fort and fighting internal enemies. "The weapons of our warfare," Paul tells us, are "mighty, through God, to the pulling down of strongholds." And one great reason why the Church is so power-

less today as a factor in the great contest with Rum, Romanism, and the tides of Anarchy is, that so much time is spent in contest with inbred sin. It is hard to carry on a civil and a foreign war at the same time. It is time that we were less conservative, and pulled down more strongholds. Christ says, "His yoke is easy and His burden light, and ye shall find rest unto your souls." And yet because of inbred sin many find it hard work to keep the commandments of God. Let morality, and culture, and moral reform (which work through the unaided will of man), repress the passions of the soul, as they often do; but let the Church of the living God, by His power be inside what they want to *appear* to be on the outside. Let us *"be* holy," for it is the great safeguard and help in *acting* holy.

3. The destruction of inbred sin is the great help to growth in grace. It removes from the heart those things that hinder growth in grace. A corn-field will grow with weeds, but better without. Inbred sin is the weed of the heart; it tempts to doubt, and then comes wavering; it tempts to proud thoughts, when there ought to be humility; and then comes struggle. Now you have had planted in your hearts the life of the Spirit, let God uproot all things that sap the energy of the soul, or distract its thought or attention.

4. The destruction of inbred sin demonstrates the power of God to save from hell. Hell is the result of sin. If a physician could not save from the disease, it would not be expected that he could save from the results. If a physician should say to a patient in Spain, suffering from cholera, "I have a sure cure; but shall have to take you to America where people do not have the disease," the patient might well hesitate and say: "If you cannot cure me where I am sick, I am afraid to take the voyage, lest I die on the passage, or lest you cannot cure me in America." If Christ cannot cure from the disease of sin in this life, how do we know He can in the life to come save us from the results of the disease? If He cannot save from sin, are we sure He can

from hell? We may well fear in that case; but when He saves now from sin, we are sure He can from hell, and we are relieved from uncertainty as regards the future. It is time that we recommended Christ in a higher degree than as an advocate who gets us free from the consequences of sin. He is a perfect physician. *Yet many look at the atonement as simply an easy way of escape from hell,* while we may go on not saved from sin. Christ died to *destroy the works of the devil,* chief of which is sin. The objection has been raised: "If inbred sin is destroyed, how can it spring up again? Would not the springing up show that it was repressed?" The answer: not at all. No state of grace is invulnerable if we do not propose to be true to God. But we will ask the objector one question. We believe Adam was created free from inbred sin. How did inbred sin find a being in him? Certainly it was not there before. Hence it is possible for tendencies to sin to spring up in a heart where once they did not exist. But let us be careful and not make "figures go on all fours," but keep to the facts.

Postscript

WE HAVE STRIVEN hitherto to avoid, as much as possible, all technical and theological terms. Suffice it to say, we have been treating in this book of the negative side of entire sanctification; namely, the destruction of inbred sin. When God has accomplished that by a stroke of Almighty power, and the heart has been made clean and pure, then He fills it with His fulness. This latter is the positive side of entire sanctification. This is what Paul exhorted the Ephesian Church to obtain. He says: "Be filled with the Spirit." The only reason that God does not fill all Christians is, that inbred sin has not been all cast out. Entire sanctification then is the fulness of God dwelling in a pure heart. It remains only now to inquire on what terms God does this work. The way to this full salvation consists of a single step, and a step to that single step.

A step to the step of *faith*; or, in other words, we must put ourselves on believing ground, and then take the step of faith. When property is for sale, it would be folly for us to believe it was our property unless we had paid the price. It is folly to trust God for a clean heart unless we are willing to let Him have His way in all respects with us. "To be, or not to be; to do, or not to do; to have, or not to have; to suffer, or not to suffer." In all things to say, "Thy will be done," regardless of people or circumstances. When we get there— when our will is wholly swallowed up in the will of God, *then the step of faith* will be as natural and as easy as to breathe; then we can easily trust God for an entirely sanctified heart. "Faithful is He that hath called you, who also will do it."

To recapitulate, then: —

1. Settle once for all and forever, that you will be true to God, by His help, every time and everywhere, up to all the light He gives you, without any mental reservation. This is consecration. This is putting yourself wholly in His hands.

2. Now believe He receives you, and doeth it, not because of any joy or emotion, but simply because He has promised to do the work when you seek Him with all the heart. The results that follow will be these. If you have *really* been sincere and in earnest, have *really* made a covenant with God, you will have confidence in your own honesty, and in the faithfulness of God to keep His part of the covenant; and *you will believe it and trust Him if He never gives you an emotional blessing as long as you live.* You will walk by naked faith. And when God sees that a real faith *habit* has been established by you,— one that does not depend on a great manifestation of His presence, but on His written agreement,— then He will come, in some way, to your heart. Usually in a deep peace. (This is the usual experience.) This is the normal state of an entirely sanctified heart. But if you expect an experience like some one else, and tease God for that, it is a sure sign that you still lack submission. You want God to save you in *your* way, and not in His own. Trust that He *doeth* it, and He will furnish you a certificate when He sees fit, that it is done. At any rate, trust God without any dictation as to *how* He is to do it. Establish the faith habit, and God will establish Himself in you.

A LIVING SACRIFICE

Preface

A FEW MONTHS AGO a brother came to the writer and asked him for some book treating upon certain phases of the subject of consecration. The writer began to look over the lists of books with which he was familiar. He found a large and rich abundance of works on holiness, but was unable to find any covering some of the vital phases of consecration.

Because many have denied the divine willingness or ability to cleanse the heart from all sin, and because others have glorified consecration as an excuse for not obtaining entire sanctification, most writers have given their especial attention to a discussion and defence of the divine side— holiness.

Therefore the writer has sought to show the human side, in a practical manner, in order to make the way plain to inquiring souls, who long to enter into "the fulness of the blessing of the gospel of Christ."

Others could have done it better, but as they have written little upon these phases of the question, the writer has endeavored to pioneer the way for the elaborate road-builder who ought to follow with greater breadth and length.

—G. A. McLaughlin

Chapter I
WHAT IS CONSECRATION?

ONSECRATION IS THE DUTY of man. Sanctification is the work of God. Neither of these two parties can do the work of the other. God, having endowed man with a free will, cannot contradict himself, by compelling human actions. Nor would there be any merit in man's actions if he were compelled. Hence God cannot consecrate us nor can he consecrate for us. Consecration is the free act of man. Since man is feeble and sin-tainted and has always failed in his efforts to cleanse himself from sin, since he has not the power to make his heart pure, only his Maker can purify his nature. One who could create such a being as man can certainly make him right again after he has fallen. Therefore God can sanctify the nature of man. These two facts kept before the mind will simplify and clear up much of the confusion that has been thrown around this subject. Man consecrates. God sanctifies. Most of the misunderstanding and false teaching on this subject originate right here. Some are expecting God to do their part, and others are endeavoring to do the divine part themselves. Some think God will consecrate them. Hence they are singing the language of a well-known hymn,

> "Consecrate me now to thy service, Lord,
>   By the power of grace divine."

But God will do nothing of the kind. He will neither repent for the sinner, nor consecrate for the saint. He never does for us what we can do for ourselves. Wherever consecration is spoken of in the word of God, it is always declared to be the act of man— not the work of God. There are others who try to take the work of God out of his hands. As the result we have a great many people who are trying to sanctify themselves. This gives rise to the theory of sanctification by culture, growth, etc. God says, "present your bodies a living sacrifice," "yield your members as instruments of righteousness as those that are alive from the dead." But he never indicates that he will present our bodies or yield our members for us. We must do that. It is true that a struggling soul, seeking to get the consent of his will, may ask God to assist him, and give him strength not to falter until the work is done, but he— not God— must perform the act of consecration. When man has done his part and consecrated himself to God entirely, then God does his part and entirely sanctifies the entirely consecrated man.

The Bible employs the marriage covenant as a symbol and illustration of consecration. Jesus Christ is represented as the bridegroom and his people are the bride. In this and all true marriage covenants the parties give themselves entirely to each other. All attachments that in anyway hinder the affection or duty of each to the other are forever sundered. All other suitors are forever discarded. The bride covenants to become the property of the groom. This is precisely the case in entire consecration. The believer separates himself entirely from every thing or person that hinders his attachment for and duty to Jesus Christ. And Jesus gave himself up entirely to and for his people: "Christ loved the Church and gave himself for it." When this covenant is truly made by the believer, God keeps his part of the covenant and cleanses the soul from all sin. We are met by the objection that it is impossible to consecrate ourselves entirely to God. But such an objection is absurd. If a bridegroom and bride can give themselves up to each other to be loyal and true, we can as really and truly give ourselves to God. If a soldier can take the oath of allegiance to the government, promising to be strictly obedient, to bear and suffer and endure whatever his superiors command, and rush into danger at the command of an officer who is liable to make mistakes and needlessly expose him to peril, and all because he has implicit confidence in the government, much more can we give ourselves into the hands of Him who never makes mistakes and who always knows what is best for us. We can do this if we believe in the divine government as truly as the soldier believes in his country. And if we love our God as truly as a patriot loves his country we will devote ourselves entirely to Him. What we can do for men, we can more easily do for God, because he promises us divine power to enable us to do it. The government furnishes arms, ammunition, clothing, food, etc., in order to make the consecration of the soldier effective. And God furnishes the spiritual equipment to make our consecration not only possible but gloriously successful. It is time that consecration be taken out of the realm of the awfully mysterious and shown to be a glorious privilege which a loving child longs to embrace. The subject has been represented as an awful thing even to think of, still more to accomplish. It ought to be just the reverse. We once heard a preacher at the close of an altar service when his people were seeking to be wholly given up to God, say, "You have done a very solemn thing to-day." To our minds, it would have been more solemn if they had refused to give themselves entirely to God.

Consecration is what we would do if it were the last day of our lives. If you knew positively that before to-morrow morning you would be in eternity, you would as a true Christian resign yourself wholly to the will of God. The language of your heart if not of your lips would be, "Into thy hands, Lord, I resign my spirit. I let go my grasp upon everything in this world." All those who get to heaven will have to be thus resigned to the will of God the last day of life. Now what a person ought to be the last day of life, he ought to be every day. Will any one then maintain that we ought to be anything else every day? Who knows that he will live all of any one day? If sudden death would be sudden glory, it will take place only in the experience of those wholly given to God. There is no excuse then for failing to be entirely consecrated to God every moment. *Whatever we ought to be we can be.* We ought to be wholly the Lord's every moment, and as we ought to be, we can be. Impossibilities are not required. We had a friend many years ago, who had a clear conversion, but was honestly perplexed over the subjects of consecration and sanctification. She was prostrated on a bed of sickness. The physician declared she must die and advised her husband to inform her of the fact. He entered the chamber and announced the sad intelligence, "The doctor says you cannot get well." Just then the door-bell rang and he went out of the room to answer the summons. Parties had come on urgent business, detaining him for quite a length of time. This announcement came as a great shock to the sufferer who had expected to recover. She questioned, "Must I give up my husband and my friends? What will become of them when I am gone?" Then the thought arose, "God is taking care of them now and can take care of them just as well when I am gone." There was a great struggle of soul for a few minutes and then she yielded herself and all she possessed entirely to God. "Instantly," as she afterwards testified, "I felt as light as a feather." This was the beginning of a richer experience than she had ever known before. She did not die. The doctor was mistaken. The writer visited her a few months later and she said, "I see now what you mean. We cannot carry the Lord in one hand and the world in the other." Here was an instance of entire consecration, by doing as if it were the last day of life. This is the secret of the triumphant deathbeds of many of the saints who had never heard the subjects of sanctification or justification definitely treated, yet who really consecrated themselves to God in the dying hour. Many sons and daughters have witnessed these deathbed scenes and asked themselves the question, "Why was not father as much given up to God every day as that last day?" Sure enough! Why not! Make the covenant with God to-day, reader! Make it regardless of your feelings! make it as you do a contract with any one in whom you have confidence in the business world! Make it whether God blesses you or not! If you will begin to do as you would if you knew it to be the last day of your life you will become entirely consecrated. A little boy once went to a camp meeting. As his mother was putting him to bed, he heard a noise in an adjacent tent. He asked what it was and his mother responded, "It is a man praying, and I judge by the way he prays that he wants to be wholly given up to the Lord." The little boy replied, "Why don't he then, mother?" We ask the same question of the many who say they want to be the Lord's, "Why not?"

Chapter II
WHO CONSECRATES?

IT IS SOMETIMES ASSERTED, "I consecrated myself to God at the time I was converted." This statement is sometimes sincerely made, but it is incorrect. No person who knows the scriptural definition of the term *consecration* will make such an assertion. *Consecration is an act which can be performed only by a child of God.* Take a reference Bible and turn to the passages that contain the words *consecration, consecrate* and their cognates and in the margin, in most instances, will be found the translation, *to fill the hand.* This refers to the method of consecration under the old dispensation. The worshipper came to the temple with his hands filled with something good to be used in the service of God — a sheaf of wheat, some of the fruits of the earth. Or he led a lamb, a goat, a heifer or a bullock. He solemnly laid his hands upon the victim and set it apart for the service of God and his sanctuary. He always brought something good for use in the service of God. This is what Paul means when he says, "Your bodies a living sacrifice, holy, acceptable unto God." God will accept nothing that is not good as a sacrifice to His service. A sinner cannot offer such a sacrifice, because he is "dead in trespasses and sins." He must be made alive by being born again before he can offer "a living sacrifice." He has nothing to give but his sins. And God has no use for them. How can a dead man offer himself, a living sacrifice! He must forsake his sins by repentance, and believe on the Lord Jesus Christ. Then he is born of God— made alive from the dead— and is in a condition to offer a *living* sacrifice. We hear men sometimes tell of giving their sins— their whiskey, tobacco, etc.— to God. How absurd! All sinful things are to be put away. They will do to burn on the devil's altar but not on the altar of God. The little slave girl in the days of oppression was ransomed from the auctioneer's block by a kind-hearted man. She fell at his feet exclaiming, "I will serve you all my life." She had been redeemed and then she consecrated to his service her redeemed powers. It is only redeemed men that have anything to consecrate. The sinner repents. The child of God consecrates. How absurd that hymn,

"All my doubts I give to Jesus."

He has no use for our doubts. Let them go where they belong. They had their origin with the devil. *A sinner is never commanded to consecrate in all the word of God.* The constant command to him is, "Repent." A reference to the word of God shows that consecration is commanded to the children of God only. In Paul's great exhortation to consecration he says (Rom. xii. 1), "I beseech you, therefore, *brethren.*" He beseeches not the unconverted, but the brethren to entirely consecrate. The epistle to the Romans was written to the *church* at Rome. In Rom. vi. 13, he repeats the same thought, "yield yourselves unto God, as those that *are alive* from the dead, and your members as instruments of righteousness unto God." Here the command to consecrate is given to those "that are alive from the dead," and not to unconverted men. If we keep this distinction in our minds, — repentance for the sinner, consecration for the child of God, — we shall avoid a fatal confusion that has hindered some good people. We must remember that every sinner is a rebel against the kingdom of heaven. And his first duty is to throw down his weapons of rebellion — in other words, repent. When people undertake to assert that repentance and consecration are the same thing, they are driven to some very absurd conclusions. We once met a brother who, in order to find an excuse for refusing to entirely consecrate himself to God, maintained stoutly that he was entirely consecrated to God *before* he was converted. If that was true, then he was a consecrated sinner, which is absurd. We once heard of a church that began a protracted meeting. For three nights the converted people were urged to come to the altar and consecrate themselves to God. Having started the meeting in this manner, the rest of the effort was an invitation to the unconverted to come to the altar and consecrate themselves to God. Both parties were exhorted to do the same thing and confusion settled down upon the minds of the people. Sinners inquired as to whether the church was unconverted, and Christians resented being asked to do the same thing that was urged upon sinners. The assertion that we consecrate when we repent is both unscriptural and illogical.

Consecration meetings in our young people's societies are never held for unconverted people, but always for those who are Christians. *Such meetings are never held for the purpose of converting sinners.* To still further substantiate this truth we call attention to the hymnals of all the denominations. In these, repentance is always adopted as the language of sinners and consecration as the language of the children of God. The language of the sinner is

> "Show pity, Lord! O Lord, forgive!
> Let a repenting rebel live:
> Are not thy mercies large and free?
> May not a sinner trust in thee?
>
> "My crimes are great, but don't surpass
> The power and glory of thy grace.
> Great God, thy nature hath no bound,
> So let thy pardoning love be found."

Such a man is like the ancient runner to the city of refuge with justice upon his track. He thinks not of the beauties of the city, but only to escape pursuing justice. Real conviction gives a man no time for anything except escape from the wrath to come. But the redeemed man expresses himself thus, as he consecrates himself to God:

> "When I survey the wondrous cross
> On which the Prince of Glory died,
> My richest gain I count but loss,
> And pour contempt on all my pride."

And the conclusion he arrives at as he reflects upon the salvation God has given him is:

> "Were the whole realm of nature mine,
> That were a present far too small;
> Love so amazing, so divine,
> Demands my soul, my life, my all."

Chapter III
COMPLETELY AND ENTIRELY

WHEN PAUL MADE HIS VOYAGE to Rome a great storm arose which threatened the loss of the ship and the lives of those on board. In order to save the ship the sailors threw overboard the wheat and other articles that composed the cargo. But later they had to cast themselves overboard also and abandon the ship. This is the way many people consecrate to God. They proceed by degrees. They yield up the less important things first, rather than give themselves. They give up prejudices or habits or their associations, money, etc., etc. They begin on the outer circumference, but self in the centre is still untouched. They keep drawing nearer to the centre, the less important things are given first and then things of greater value, but still they are not consecrated, until they come to self and give that. Then the consecration is complete. They commenced at the wrong place. Had they commenced with self in the beginning everything else would have gone with it. Giving money, time and effort is only trying to get salvation by works until self is given. Then these things go with the consecration, just as the first link draws all the chain with it. Consecration must be complete, and it is never complete until the whole being is given to God.

Paul says, "Your bodies, a living sacrifice." We used to wonder why he said "your bodies" and said nothing as regards the soul. But we think we see the reason of it now. The body is the instrument through which the soul works. The soul is useless in this world without a body, and can accomplish nothing except through the body. A consecration that is simply in the mind is mere sentiment. And we have too much of that in our day. Consecration must be practical. It cannot be if the body is left out. There is more danger in sentimental consecration that leaves out the body than anything else as regards this question. A great many claim to be consecrated who are not, for this reason. The word of God teaches that consecration is to be intensely practical. We have a body as truly to be consecrated as the soul. The two cannot be separated and be of any use in this world. Disembodied spirits of men are of no use to God here below. It is only for the little season while we are in the body that we can be useful here. There is a legal instrument in the courts called the *habeas corpus*, meaning, "*you may have his body.*" A man may by the granting of this writ be brought into court and allowed to show whether he has been justly shut up in jail or not. When his body is brought into court, his soul and spirit are there too, they all go together. The soul is not left behind in the jail. The whole man is there. It seems to us that the apostle meant all this; that the soul is of no use without the body in this world and the body is necessary to make the desire and purpose of consecration practical and complete. Otherwise consecration is of no account in building up the kingdom of God on earth. When the Jewish high priest was consecrated to his sacred office the blood of the sacrifice was touched upon his right ear, the thumb of his right hand, and the great

toe of his right foot, to teach that his ears were to be attentive to hear the commands of God; his hands ready to do
the work God commanded; and his feet quick to run on
the divine errands. In this dispensation all believers are "a
royal priesthood." Their bodies are to be given to a living
service. The ears are to be attentive to the divine commands; the hands to do the bidding of God and the feet to
run on His errands. The whole body is to be kept in such a
manner that the soul can best serve the kingdom of God.
Anything that weakens or impairs the body hinders the
best service of the soul and is to be avoided, for our "bodies are the temples of the Holy Ghost," and God says, "If
any man defile the temple of God, him shall God destroy."
Sloth, intemperance and unchastity are to be discarded that
the soul may be unhindered in its duty and devotion to
God. Jesus once dwelt in a human body and henceforth
the body is to be prized as that abode in which he conde-
scended to dwell. Those blessed eyes beamed with looks of
love and tenderness towards the erring. They shed tears
over the grave of Lazarus and the incorrigible city of Jerusa-
lem. His ear was quick to distinguish his Father's voice
when the dull ears of the multitude heard only an incom-
prehensible sound. His tongue spoke forth the praises of
his Father. His hands were employed in doing good to
mankind all through his ministry, and when he was received up into heaven his hands were spread in blessing
upon a ruined world. But he is no longer in a human body
upon earth. He has gone up to heaven and we are to be his
body. We are to have our bodies take the place of his body
here upon earth. Hence the church is the body of which he
is the head. He is now to work through our bodies. The
world no longer sees him, but it sees us. He still manifests
himself, but it is through his church. Our ears must be
quick and ready to hear the divine commands; our voices
must be tuned to speak forth the Father's praises, just as
his voice once did; our hands must take his place in doing

good; our feet must gladly run on errands for God; our whole body, as the expression of our entire nature, must be a living sacrifice to do, be or suffer the will of God, for we now take the place of Jesus as the representatives of God upon earth. How absurd in the light of this truth are those isms and fanatical notions that slight or neglect the body!

In later years there has arisen an absurdity that has captured some weak souls called "Christian Science." (Was there ever a fanaticism that did not try to appropriate the name of Christ to find excuse for its existence?) Its fundamental philosophy is that there is no such thing as matter, that everything is mind. It is the old heathen notion of Pantheism revamped. But the inspired word of God declares that we have a body as well as a soul and spirit to be offered to God. Paul prayed that "your whole spirit and soul and *body* be preserved blameless unto the coming of our Lord Jesus Christ."

Another absurdity which has swept many weak souls to destruction is Spiritism, which makes a man good for nothing while in the body, but makes him very benevolently anxious to communicate with the living after he is dead. But no good ever came of these pretended communications. There never was a man made better by them or saved thereby from sin, which is enough to show that it is not of God. But God wants us to be good for something while we are alive and not merely after we are dead. He wants a consecration while in the body; a practical, complete offering only is of any consequence to God or man in its results. Christianity has given more honor to the body than any other religion because the body is the instrument of the soul, the temple of the Holy Ghost, and without it the soul can accomplish nothing. Hence instead of leaving it out of the question as being the grosser part of our nature, the consecration takes it in also. Thus the last and least of us is to be offered to God— a complete consecration of all our being.

Chapter IV
COMPLETED ONCE FOR ALL

C ONSECRATION IS NOT ONLY COMPLETE as embracing the whole man, but it is to be completed once for all. So it does not need to be done every day, but done once for all, like any other transaction that involves a contract. This may be seen in the very nature of consecration. It is the marriage covenant between Jesus Christ and his church. A true marriage is a permanent contract between two parties. It is made once for all. And nothing but death or infidelity to the contract can break it. The modern innovation of consecration meetings once a month is as absurd and as impotent as would be a marriage ceremony celebrated once a month between the same parties. In his word God speaks of nothing short of an everlasting covenant, never to be broken. He says, "I will make with thee an everlasting covenant." Until the believer understands this he will ever be at a disadvantage in contending against the temptations of Satan. Until he has got the matter forever fixed, as positively and definitely as a wedding day and its vows, he will be a prey to the temptations of

Satan, who will tempt him on the point of his emotions and feelings. He will be tempted to think that he is not saved because he does not feel as at some other time, or as some one else feels, or as he expected he would feel. But when he has once settled the matter to be unreservedly the Lord's, he can in the fierceness of temptation declare that he is entirely given up to God since that day, he has taken nothing back and is wholly the Lord's, no matter what the enemy may say or suggest. We shall refer to this point again. We can never get quite to the point of a complete consecration until we get this covenant signed and sealed once for all, for a very good reason: when the same individuals come to the altar again and again for a consecration which they expect to go all over again at a stated interval, they never get the consecration complete, because "the old man" dies hard. If there be an idol we do not quite want to destroy, a Benjamin or Isaac that we do not wish to part with, the temptation is to defer the matter until "a more convenient season." This is in accordance with human nature: to put off disagreeable things as long as possible. The "old man" will put off entire consecration just as long as he can because it means death to him. We have heard leaders at camp meeting ask all who would consecrate themselves to God "for this camp meeting" to come to the altar for that purpose. How about the next week when the camp meeting is over? how about the time when the protracted meeting ceases? ought we not to be entirely the Lord's all the time? Is it not presumption to even suggest the idea that God will accept short-time consecration? And yet there are many churches who feel the need of the Holy Ghost for the winter revival season, who consecrate for that brief period, as they suppose, but it is only a religious spasm and not a scriptural consecration.

But it has been asked, "How shall we know when we have made this complete consecration?" We reply, when we have given ourselves to God the very best we know and are so anxious to give all we do not know, that we would be real glad to have God tell us what more we can be or do for him, then we are entirely his. The angels in heaven can do no more than to give up themselves as well as they know and be willing and eager for God to show them anything lacking so that they may yield it to him. When two souls stand before the altar and pledge their love and devotion each to the other, it is not only for the present but for all time, "for sickness or health, prosperity and adversity." It is for all the unknown future. The part that is unknown is bigger than that which is known. So with consecration, it is for the unknown future as well as the present. When new duties come up in the future or new leadings of Providence or new opportunities of being the Lord's, we are simply carrying out the covenant once and forever made. God will give us new light as we go along. We were not capable of receiving all the light at the start, but he accepts the will for the deed and opens new fields of privilege and opportunity and duty as fast as we can bear it.

When the expedition under General Butler sailed from New York during the late Civil War, sealed orders were given them, which were not to be opened until they had been several days at sea. On opening the orders, on the appointed day, they found they were commanded to go to the mouth of the Mississippi and take New Orleans. There was no shrinking or drawing back, for the soldiers had taken the oath when mustered into the service of the United States, binding them to loyalty and strict obedience. Therefore they went gladly to the task set before them. Every entirely consecrated Christian gives himself up to go and do and be and suffer as God says. He has sworn allegiance to the government of heaven, and he is ready for the un-known will of God as fast as God reveals it to him.

Here is where the "old man" draws back, afraid of be-ing injured. But any shrinking here is for one of two rea-sons: either from a doubt of the goodness or the wisdom of God. Some doubt the wisdom of God and are fearful that he may call them to something that is not the very best thing for them after all. There is an element of self-conceit here in thinking they know better than God. Most unbe-lief comes from self-conceit.

Others doubt the goodness of God; they fear that if they give up to him unreservedly something terrible would hap-pen. The devil tells many people that if they are wholly given up to God, they will be treated meanly. Somebody will die, or they will be sick or lose their friends. He makes them believe that God will punish them for being good and that the more obedient they are the more they must suffer. There are some people who actually seem to think that it is unhealthy and even dangerous to be very good. That it is a sign that we shall soon be called to die. Their idea of saintliness is a pale, bloodless face, a consumptive frame and a soul just ready to depart from this wicked world. The Sunday-school books we read when a child had the unhappy custom of allowing the good boys to die young, and the idea is instilled in many minds too much that to be real good means to have a real sad, gloomy time of it. There are people still who believe that if we are real good and entirely submissive to God that he will take an unfair advantage of us and treat us meanly.

He who believes in the perfect wisdom and infinite good-ness of Almighty God will trust his whole case in the divine keeping, for the present and the future, for time and eter-nity. He who wants to cling to unbelief and the self life will make excuses and find an excuse for keeping back part of the price.

Some pretend not to see any need of entire sanctification, after a man has been soundly converted, and stoutly maintain that we are entirely sanctified when regenerated. If we are entirely sanctified when converted, then there should not be the least shrinking from entire consecration. The very fact that men do shrink from being entirely given up to God proves that there needs to be another work of divine grace to remove this unwillingness to be or do or suffer all the will of God.

Chapter V
NOT TO THE CHURCH

WE HEAR MUCH SAID in many quarters about "loyalty to the church," but it pains us to hear very little said about loyalty to Jesus Christ. We do not believe in "Come-out-ism." God has blessed organized effort all through the ages, while "Come-out-ism" has ruined many souls. This ism pretends to disbelieve in sects, but is really one of the most intolerant and bigoted of all the sects. For it is a little partially organized sect of its own, that devotes itself to chastisement of the churches, to whom it owes all the religious light and life that it possesses. Had the world been dependent for its moral and spiritual light upon this absurd principle, it would have perished in ignorance of the gospel. The Bible, the Sabbath, the sanctuary and vital religion have come down to us through regular organized efforts of the people of God, banded together for this purpose. If the church is not all it should be, instead of drawing off from it we should remain in it and live a holy life and seek to make it better. "Ye are the salt of the earth," said Jesus, concerning his true people. Salt can accomplish its purpose best by remaining in contact with that which needs to be purified. "Ye are the light of the world," said Jesus. And again he says, "Neither do men light a candle and put it under a bushel, but on a candlestick; and it giveth light unto all that are in the house." God wants all that are in his house— the church— to receive the benefit of every experience given by him to individuals. We have said this because we do not wish to be misunderstood when we say that there is great danger in these days *in being consecrated to the church more than to the Lord*. While church organization is a necessity and membership in it a privilege and a duty, there is great danger of being consecrated to the organization more than to God. There are strange ideas in vogue as to Christian work. We have been astonished to hear certain people called great Christian workers. When we came to investigate their special work it was the preparation of church suppers, the piecing of quilts and dressing dolls for the church bazaar. Many a so-called Christian worker is dumb in the social means of grace, knows little of the word of God and would not know how to pray with a dying man or how to point a sinner to Christ. It has come to pass that a person can be "a devoted Christian worker" and have no salvation at all, or if there is salvation in the heart there is no way of finding it out. Much that passes for Christian work is "serving tables" to keep alive five or six little denominations in a community where one could do all the work of God if it were "filled with the Spirit." We knew of a sister who was relating her experience of restoration to health. She declared that in her gratitude to God, she was now working specially for Him. Being questioned as to the special work she was now doing replied, "I am going around soliciting articles

for a fish-pond to be held at the parsonage next Thurs-
day night." For the benefit of those of our readers
who do not know what a fish-pond is, we would say
it is a kind of pious gambling. We have known of men
who were very liberal to the church as long as they
could have their way, but when things did not go to
suit them, they backslid and left the church and went
into the service of Satan. Their excuse was that they
were "not appreciated" after all they had done for
the church. They were laboring only for self or the
applause of the people. Had they been consecrated
to God, they would not have cared for or desired the
applause of men. There is much that passes for
Christian work that has no more of the spirit of Christ
than of Mohammed. Many churches are run like a
political machine, just to keep up with the others in
the community without regard to the glory of God.
Churches may be managed with such a spirit as to
hinder true Christianity. Much so-called religious
work may be done without one spark of spiritual life.
We were pressing the claims of God upon a worldly
professor of Christianity who was candid enough to
acknowledge, "If I was as good a Christian as I am a
Methodist, I would be getting along all right." Not
that we would have people one whit the less devoted
to building up the cause of God, but we insist that
consecration is to be to God first and then to his visible church. Soldiers are consecrated to the cause of
their country first, then to their individual regiment.
Otherwise petty quarrels and jealousies would destroy any army. Jesus first, then our denomination
as the best method of building up the cause of Jesus
upon earth. Paul says, "He is the head of the body,
the church:… that in all things he might have the pre-
eminence." This being true, a man may be consecrated to God and be misunderstood by the visible

church. In fact the visible church has not usually in the past understood many of its best members, who were living for God. Sometimes they have been cast out because not comprehended nor appreciated. A fully consecrated man is like Jesus, willing to suffer reproaches even from those he is endeavoring to benefit. But being thoroughly consecrated to God, he does not waver. Here is where some weaken, they let their fear of man or desire for human applause weaken and nullify the voice of conscience. Instead of being consecrated to God they let other people control their consciences and mark out their duty and then wonder why they have so little religious joy and comfort. The difficulty is, they are not consecrated to God, but to the people. Here is where many draw back to-day. They have not given their reputations to God. They fear what people may say of them, especially good people. Sometimes we have to be misunderstood by good people. The church may misunderstand us. But our first duty is to God. We must be what he wishes us to be; not what the church wishes always. Jesus and many of the best of the saints have been misunderstood by the church. The church-men of His day clamored for his crucifixion. And if they clamor for our crucifixion, we need not be astonished. A hymn is very popular that contains the lines:

"Let the world despise and leave me:
  They have left my Saviour, too."

But it may be equally true:

"Let the church despise and leave me:
  They have left my Saviour, too."

Good men, sincere men, may, through prejudice, misunderstand us, but we must go with Jesus just the same and keep sweet towards them. We are following a master who made himself of no reputation. Here is the point where many draw back and do not go through to God. They are trying to save their reputation. John Wesley was bitterly attacked by his enemies. His brother Charles told him that he had better write a tract showing the falsity of the charges, which he could easily do. He replied that he had made a series of daily appointments to preach the gospel in the north of England and in Scotland, and if he stopped at home to repel the attacks of his enemies, the people would not hear the gospel. "I gave my reputation to the Lord many years ago and he will have to take care of it now." He went right away and left his reputation in the hands of God and it has kept well for over a hundred years, because it had a good keeper. Would the reader dare to do that? Those who are so fearful about their reputation usually do not have a reputation worth worrying about.

Right here may be mentioned the reason so many have a weak faith in God. Jesus states it. He preached the most systematic of all his discourses, clearly proving his divinity. His Unitarian hearers said they did not believe it. He replied, "How can ye believe, which receive honor one of another, and seek not the honor that cometh from God only?" It is impossible to trust God when we care more for the opinions of men than for his opinion. Here is the point where self centres, but if we get the consent of our hearts to die to the opinions of those who would hinder our supreme loyalty to God, we shall surely get great victory. Have you given your reputation to God or are you concerned about it when the question of loyalty to God presents itself?

Chapter VI
MORE THAN FOR SERVICE

A NOTHER POPULAR NOTION IS "consecration to work" in order to obtain "power for service." This idea dwarfs and belittles consecration, making it only human doing. Consecration is more than doing. In fact doing is a very small part of it. It means *to be, to do, and to suffer the will of God*— all three. Sometimes it is easier to do the will of God than to be what we ought to be, or to suffer the will of God. We have heard old soldiers say that it took more courage and firmness to lie still under the fire of the enemy than to rush into the thickest of the fight. It is easier to do than to suffer. God calls us to both. Those who are putting emphasis upon "consecration for work" do not recognize the fact that God cares more for what we are than for what we do. He is seeking to fully stamp his image upon the soul. He cares more for character than for conquest. He declares in his word, "He that is slow to anger is better than the mighty; and he that ruleth his spirit than he that taketh a city." Most people had rather take a city than rule their own spirit. It is more pleasing to be a great conqueror, whose name is exalted among the people, than to rule the spirit. It exalts the self-life to be called a great saint, a wonderful preacher, a noted evangelist. Many a man passes for a great spiritual leader who is far from being consecrated to God. There may be a great deal of self mixed with the thought of getting "power for service," with the idea of self-exaltation in it all; the desire to make ourselves some great one instead of possessing the lowly graces of a holy character. This was the case with Simon Magus. He wanted to buy the Holy Ghost power so that he could work miracles. He offered money, while some to- day offer their consecration to buy the power of the Holy Ghost. Some one says that seeking the Holy Ghost just to get power for service is like a man marrying his housekeeper not from love, but because it is cheaper and he can save by it. He who obtains the gift of the Holy Ghost obtains him first in his abiding fulness, not in order to get his help, but from a love that desires his constant companionship. There are thousands willing to be illustrious in the church, through the help of the Holy Spirit, who are unwilling to be holy through his abiding presence. God is seeking lowly character. He delights to dwell with him that is of a contrite heart. It may be the Lord wants you to be a perfect, patient Job to shame the devil and let him know that God has those who are ready to suffer his will. If consecration were only to do, and to have power for service, were we banished like John in Patmos, where we could do nothing, we would be tempted to think that we had lost our salvation. All John could do was to be "in the spirit" and listen to what God had to teach him. It requires a higher degree of grace to be in the nursery with cross children, as many a mother has to be, and keep patient, than it does to stand on the walls of Zion and blow a big trumpet. Holy character is the mightiest power in this universe. Paul declares that although he might have the eloquence of men and angels combined, the power to penetrate into all mysteries, the ability to move mountains because of his great faith, the possession of a liberality that sacrificed everything, and yet if he failed to be clothed with the lowly garment of perfect love, he would amount to nothing. Purity is power in itself. A holy man or woman has a character that penetrates and moves society wherever they dwell. Seeking for power amounts to nothing. No man ever got power by seeking it. And yet it is possible to get great crowds to come to the altar seeking power for service, while very few can be persuaded to seek purity of heart, the real condition of power.

The popular notion of power is entirely different from the power of purity. A great deal of the seeking for power is a seeking for a kind of misty, intangible something that is expected to come over the seeking soul and compel him to do certain duties which he is not quite willing to do, just as a tyrant has to drag a subject up to an unwelcome task. Some people think to be full of power is to be like a great reservoir full and slopping over, and that it puts a kind of gush in us that enables us to do hard, disagreeable things because of the gush. There never was a greater mistake. God does not want great reservoirs. He wants clear, empty channels through which he can pour himself out on a lost world. If we will keep ourselves clean, empty channels he will flow through us to the world about us. He wants insulated wires. If we will be insulated, separated entirely from the world, he will turn his divine power through us on the world all about us. When we are wholly given up to him, we will do or speak or suffer or be, entirely regardless of any particular gush of emotion. We shall not stop to ask how we feel or whether duty is easy or hard. He has genuine power who is so yielded to God that God can shine through him upon the world. And many times he is accomplishing most when he himself realizes it least. Let us disabuse our minds of the idea that the froth and foam and bustle and noise are power. Sometimes they are tokens of feebleness. The power that keeps the locomotive on the track is mightier than the power that speeds it along the track. The latter is the power of steam. The former is the power of gravitation that holds the planets in their places. The power that can keep us from flying the track, that can keep us sweet and true to God, is greater than the power that helps us blow the whistle and ring the bell. There are many people who would like the power to suffer and be humble if some one could only know it and give them credit for it.

It may be objected here that we imply that it is not of importance that we are zealous workers for God. We intend to convey no such idea. We do mean that work is not of the most consequence. Character comes first in the teachings of the sacred scriptures. God gives us salvation; then we are to work it out. We are to *be* first of all, then we shall *do*. Being right is a great help to doing right. Christ died that he "might purify unto himself a peculiar people zealous of good works." We see here then that when our character is what he wants it, and he has purified us, then we shall be "zealous of good works." This then is the order — purity of character, then zeal for good works. The first command is *"Be"* — "Be ye holy." When we are what he wants us to be, we shall do all he wants us to do. Then he can take our little and feed a great multitude. There need be no fear of our being without power when we are wholly consecrated to be, do and suffer the will of God. Some one says that "God can thresh a mountain with a worm." This is true. The reason he does not thresh more mountains is because there are so few willing to be worms. So many want to be great. It is only when we get small enough and weak enough that God will use us. Here is where so many fall into the snare of wanting to be great. More evangelists and preachers have become powerless here than at any other point. They sought power in order to show off. If we would not be ensnared right here, let us be sure we are consecrated to be, to do and to suffer the will of God.

Then we shall not be elated by success, nor cast down by apparent failure, because we have given all the glory to God. God says he will not share his glory with another, and many are trying to rival him. The word of God does not command consecration for service or to work— *but to God.*

Chapter VII
NOT TO OUR FEELINGS

MANY PEOPLE ARE CONSECRATED to their feelings and emotions more than to God. They have come to estimate their religious state by the amount of "good feelings" they have. When they feel bad, they think they have no religion; when they feel well they suppose it is an indication of the possession of very much grace. Some of these people think very little about their conduct and character but very much of their feelings. Whether they live right or not does not concern them very much, but they are very much disturbed if they do not "feel good." This is one of the weaknesses of modern religion. People are seeking frames and feelings more than God. Such religion is mere sentiment, and so far has it gone that the majority of seekers at the altars of religion, whether it be for pardon or heart-purity, are seeking more an emotional experience than a radical change of character. They want to feel good more than they want to be good. They object to radical treatment that destroys sin, because it requires too much self-abasement and crucifixion. A little boy of our acquaintance a few years ago fell out of a hammock and broke his arm. When the physician came to set the bones, the little fellow appealed to his mother saying, "Don't let him do it, mamma. Give me medicine; give me medicine." There are many in the church who had rather have soothing medicine than to have their bones set and made right. About all some preachers dare to deal out is soothing syrup. Many want to feel nice whether they are right or not. The result is a large class of religious weaklings. They seek the loaves and fishes of religion instead of righteousness. Feeling is not religion, but it is the result of true religion. Many want the results who do not desire the cause— salvation. Here is the great vantage ground of Satan. He harasses many good people right at this point and gets the advantage over them and destroys their souls. Perhaps there is no more common form of Satanic attack than right here. It is not too much to say that every Christian has had more or less trouble right at this point. The will is the only possession that man can call his own. God can touch and modify and destroy everything else. Property, friends, health, life are at his disposal, but our will is at our own disposal. He will never violate the freedom of our will. He will not break our will. We are our own governors when it comes to the freedom of the will. We can exercise the power of choice but we cannot control our feelings and emotions. He alone can do that. He can touch and thrill them as a musician controls the strings of his instrument. Hence the control of the will belongs to us. The state of our emotions and feelings belongs to him. It is our business to be firm in our determination to be entirely his and he will give us joy and peace or allow "heaviness through manifold temptations," to suit himself.

This is the last thing that many people give up who are

trying to consecrate themselves to God. It is a common experience to hear people say, "I am all the Lord's but I do not feel any different." This very expression goes to prove that they are not wholly given up to God. If they were wholly given to him, they would be given up in the matter of their emotions, frames and feelings. When wholly given up to God, we shall be content to feel as he wishes. The desire for some remarkable manifestation in our experience comes from a wilfulness, whereby we desire our own way instead of God's way. Many people linger about our altars seeking justification or entire sanctification who never obtain either because they want God to come to their terms and save them in their way and not in his way. And such people, although they may think they have consecrated a great many things to the Lord, are leagues distant from entire consecration because they have not given their feelings to him. Reader, if you have been seeking in vain "the fulness of the blessing" stop and ask yourself if the cause of your failure is not because you have expected God to save you in your own way instead of allowing him to save you in his way.

Taking this view of consecration we shall have great vantage ground to withstand the attacks of Satan. When he tells us that we do not feel as we should, we can reply, "I belong wholly to the Lord." When he asserts that we do not feel like other people, we can maintain that we "belong to the Lord wholly," and that we accept none of his suggestions and believe none of his insinuations: that he must bring forth facts or we will not believe him. Keep declaring and maintaining, "I belong to God," no matter what may be your feelings or fancies. Go by your facts. You have made a covenant with God and have taken nothing back and are keeping your part of the contract the best you know. Act just as people do in the business world. They do not successfully do business on their feelings, but on their facts. A man who has sufficient money in the bank but stops his business because he *feels* poor is a fool. And are people much better who have truly given all to God and then allow the devil to persuade them to cast away their confidence because they do not feel after a certain way or manner! It is time people were taught to estimate the degree of their religion, not by their feelings, but by the spirit in which they endure the trials of life. We have dwelt at length on this point because here is the turning point in the spiritual experience of thousands. No man ever becomes a perfect Christian until he has learned the happy method of maintaining his contract in spite of his feelings. The way to become established is to let this become *a habit*.

Let no one suppose that we discount or disapprove of a religion of the emotions. We believe in and enjoy such a religious experience, but we enjoy it, not because we seek to be happy, but because we have the salvation from which flows the joy of the Holy Ghost.

Chapter VIII
With Certainty

"BUT HOW MAY I KNOW when I am wholly consecrated to God?" is the question often asked. There are many who do not know whether they are entirely the Lord's or not. There is so such uncertainty in some quarters that it has actually voiced itself in this query of a hymn,

"Am I His, or am I not?"

We once asked a sister coming from a service if she was wholly the Lord's. The reply was, "I do not know." Being told that this was a matter that she ought to know for herself, she said, "Ask our minister."

A wholly consecrated soul will know that it is a fact without having to ask preacher, priest or bishop. If we do not know that we are wholly the Lord's, we are not wholly the Lord's. He who has settled this matter knows it, just as really as he knows anything in this world. He has two witnesses to his consecration.

First, he has the witness of his own spirit— the consciousness that the matter is forever settled, the great transaction is done. We know this the same way that we know we have

decided on any other transaction. If we have been in doubt
about buying a piece of property, but have finally decided
to purchase it and announce ourselves as ready and willing to fulfil all the conditions and lay the money down, we
know we have done it. If there are future conditions which
we cannot now fulfil and are not required of us until some
future time, if we have decided in advance to fulfil them,
we know we have thus decided. And if we give ourselves
thus to God— all we know and all we do not know— we
certainly know we have done it. Consecration is a business
transaction between us and God. Any one who knows how
to do honest business, knows how to consecrate himself to
God. And no one yet ever honestly made the full covenant
with God, no matter if he did it without any emotion, just
as he would do any business with a party in whom he had
confidence, without finding it to be the gateway to a new,
richer and more glorious experience.

Second, we may know it by the testimony of the Holy
Spirit. The object and end of consecration being entire sanctification (see next chapter), the latter should follow as soon
as the consecration is made complete. To this work of entire sanctification the Holy Spirit witnesses. Thus he becomes a witness, not only to our entire sanctification, but
naturally also to our consecration which precedes it. Consecration is our work; to this we have the direct witness of
our own spirit. Sanctification is God's work to which he
witnesses, and in thus witnessing to his own work, he witnesses to ours, for he cannot sanctify us till we are wholly
consecrated. This is the completeness of the test. The first
evidence (of our own spirit) must be supplemented by the
testimony of the Holy Spirit. To think we had the testimony of our spirit, without the testimony of the Holy Spirit,
is presumption based upon self-deception. To think we have
the testimony of the Spirit, on account of some feeling or
emotion, if we have not the testimony of our own spirit
that we have given ourselves to God, is fanaticism. It is the

office of the Holy Spirit to witness to every instalment of grace that is given. Jesus said that the Holy Spirit was not only the Comforter, but the Comforter that *witnesses*. When Daguerre was perfecting the process of portrait making by means of the camera, which has revolution- ized that art, he found it impossible to retain the picture upon the glass slide. As soon as it was drawn out into the light, the picture vanished. After experimenting for a time he spread a coating of chemicals upon the glass and then drew it out in a dark slide, and in a dark closet with other chemicals fixed the image on the glass to stay. There are a great many who waver in their consecration. They get there and stay a little while and then recede. What we need to do is to wait until God comes, sanctifies and seals us by the witness of the Spirit and enables us to make our consecra- tion permanent. When Abraham made his covenant, he sat down and watched it, keeping away the unclean birds until the burning lamp and smoking furnace attested by their appearance that the sacrifice was accepted and hence complete. So Paul says we are to present our bodies a liv- ing sacrifice in order that we "*may prove* what is that good and acceptable and perfect will of God." When we get this divine proof from God by the witnessing Spirit, then we know that the consecration is complete.

Many are confused over the witness of the Spirit. Some are looking for great manifestations of glory, rapturous visions, etc. But the witness of the Spirit is an inward per- suasion, wrought by the Holy Spirit, that the work is com- plete. It may have no great, miraculous manifestations at all. This is indescribable. It is the white stone with the new name which no man can read save he who possesses it. Until we have this comfortable persuasion, we can never be sure that we are wholly consecrated to God. Reader, if you have not yet "proved what is that good and accept- able and perfect will of God," it is surely because you have not given up to him wholly. You are holding on to something. If you do not know what it is, then guess at it and ask God to help you in your conjecture. If you are honest he will show you, if you are real anxious to know.

Many are not wholly consecrated because they are seeking a blessing merely; others because they have marked out a certain way for God to come and bless them— in their way instead of his way. Some are thinking their consecration will buy sanctification and are trying to be saved by its merit. Very many are not consecrated because they fear what the people will say. They are trying to take care of their reputation themselves instead of giving it to God. Very few are willing to be of no reputation for Jesus' sake. If the holy fire has not yet fallen upon the sacrifice, find out at what point you have failed to put it all on the altar. If you really want to know at any cost, the Spirit will surely tell you. "And if in anything ye be otherwise minded, God shall reveal even thus unto you."

Chapter IX
FOR A PURPOSE

WHEN GOD COMMANDS sinners to repent it is always for a definite purpose— that their sins may be forgiven, and he cannot consistently forgive sins unless there is real repentance. Peter said on the day of Pentecost, "Repent and be baptized every one of you for the remission of sins." Another day he said to the assembled multitude, "Repent ye therefore and be converted, that your sins may be blotted out." We have shown in a previous chapter that repentance is no more the duty of a sinner than consecration is the duty of the child of God. And the consecration of the child of God is as truly for a definite purpose as is the repentance of the sinner. The sinner repents in order to be pardoned. The child of God consecrates in order to be entirely sanctified— completely conformed to the will and image of God. When we are entirely consecrated to God then he entirely sanctifies us, because it is impossible to conceive of any thing or person belonging wholly to God and being impure. He has no impurity in his possession. All that is his is free from sin.

This is the reason so many people consecrate and consecrate (as they think they do) and it amounts to nothing. They get no uplift in their experience, no victory. Their consecration amounts to nothing. They do not have heart-purity as the definite end and purpose of their consecration. We find that talk of consecration is very popular to-day, but talk about entire sanctification is very unpopular. It is very common to hear people say, "I am wholly the Lord's, I am consecrated but I am not sanctified." There seems to be a delight, a kind of glorying in what they have done, but a hesitation to say anything about what God has done. It is as much as to say, "I have done it all. God has not done his part." Much of the talk about consecration is only self-glorification. This is the reason that consecration meetings are popular, while holiness meetings are unpopular. The carnal nature delights in what we do, but shrinks from that act of God whereby he makes us holy, because it means death to the old man. If the reader doubts this let him note carefully the testimonies he hears, how glibly the tongue will run over the term "consecration" and how it will hesitate at "sanctification," though the former word is used but a few times in the word of God, while the latter is constantly found in its pages. *The consecration of those who do not thereby seek to be entirely sanctified amounts to little.*

We see in this light the mistake of those who consecrate only for a good feeling or emotion, or in order to be more successful workers. We sometimes hear it said of consecration, "I did that when I had my call to the ministry. I consecrated myself to the ministry." That is another matter entirely. Many consecrations to the ministry are simply a yielding up of stubbornness and rebellion, a willingness henceforth to be obedient. But as we showed in Chapter VI, consecration is more than to do. It is to be and suffer also. God calls all men to consecrate in order to purity. He commands only a few to consecrate themselves to the special work of the ministry.

When the seven deacons were chosen for their special work, they had already been entirely consecrated to God. They were men "full of the Holy Ghost and wisdom." Men may, and have been, consecrated to the ministry who were not consecrated to God. But a person who has once for all made a complete consecration of himself to God, and is then called to the ministry, recognizes the call to the ministry as only a part of the great final consecration he made at the beginning. We cannot see all the details, but as fast as God shows them we are to recognize them as part of the original contract, whether it be to be a preacher or fulfil the duties of a humble layman. The object of erecting an altar and placing a sacrifice upon it in ancient times was to have a fire upon it. All altars that have a true, complete sacrifice upon them draw fire from heaven. When the offering was wholly placed upon the altar at the dedication of the tabernacle then down came the fire upon it. So also at the dedication of Solomon's temple. And so, too, when our consecration is complete. Of what use is an altar without fire and of what use a consecration that does not draw fire from heaven? If we have not yet received the fire, depend upon it the consecration is defective.

Chapter X
WHY SHOULD WE CONSECRATE?

THE FIRST GREAT REASON given by Paul is because it is "your reasonable service." Not because you can be more useful (although that is true) but because it is a duty that is reasonable. It is reasonable that after God has done so much for us we should be entirely his. There is nothing more unreasonable than to keep anything back from him. Since he has redeemed us from the power of the enemy, and dignified us by allowing us to be called by his name, as his children, there is no good reason or excuse for withholding any "part or parcel" of our whole being from him.

Paul makes exhortation from the mercies of God. "By the mercies of God," he says. Mercy has so strewed our path in life with blessings. It has been as David says, a "multitude of tender mercies." As free as the air we breathe; as abundant as the light of the sun that bathes the earth; as freely flowing as the water we drink is the continued stream of divine mercies. Mercy grieved over our youthful sins and follies; mercy rejoiced when we came to God in repentance and sought forgiveness of sins; mercy wept when we made our "crooked paths and shortcomings"; mercy hung on the cross and died for us; mercy has ascended to heaven and pleads there for us. It has been mercy, mercy every day, since we first breathed the air of heaven. Yet some of us hesitate and make excuses for not being wholly consecrated to God! We want to keep back part of the price. We act in this matter as if it were an unreasonable, ungrateful task, when God says it is a reasonable service! Is it not strange! There is nothing more ungrateful in the universe than the human heart! After God has done so much for us! He has done more for us than for the angels, and yet we make all manner of excuses to avoid consecrating ourselves entirely to him!

A good many act as if they expected to be hurt, if they let God have them entirely. They say or think, "If I give up entirely to Him, something dreadful might happen. Some one in the home might die, or I might be laid on a bed of sickness, or lose my property or have some other affliction." How absurd! Will God punish us for being good? Is that the kind of God you worship? Can you take better care of yourself than God can? Can he not take away everything if you do not yield to him? Do you worship a God that is too wise to make any mistakes with you and too good to be unkind? or do you worship a God who is a creature of your own fashioning? Do you punish your children for being good and judge Him by yourself? The fact that you hesitate and make excuses for keeping back part of the price, refusing to yield up entirely to the care and keeping of your best friend, shows that there is need of a further work of grace; that there is something in you that needs to die. It is the carnal nature. God says it is "your reasonable service," but by your excuses, you seek to prove that it is unreasonable. If there were no other reason why we need to be entirely sanctified, we could see it in this inward disposition that shrinks and fears it will be hurt, if we let the dear Lord that bought us have us wholly. Man made in the image of God is the only creature on the face of the earth that refuses to do the will of God. And the most inconsistent of all men is the man who is trying to serve God and keeps back a part of the price.

It is a great consolation in adversity and trial to know that we are the Lord's property— his saints. He says in Psalm 50.5: "Gather my saints together unto me; those that have made a covenant with me by sacrifice." Those who have given themselves to Him, a living sacrifice, are his saints. And there is great consolation in knowing we are his. There will be times when every true man will be called to take a stand for righteousness and holiness when he will perhaps be in the minority, misunderstood and maligned. What a consolation then to know that we are the Lord's property, and that he is taking care of his property; that nothing shall come to harm us except what he permits, and that he will never leave nor forsake his property. When consecration has become a reality to us then it will make no difference with us whether we live or die. If we live, we have the Lord's presence with us in this world. If we die, we go to dwell with him in "the more excellent glory." Living or dying we are the Lord's. We belong to ourselves no more. The United States government has provided national homes for the old soldiers who gave themselves for the defence of the nation. There everything has been done for the comfort of the veteran. His last days are free from care. He need not worry about his food, raiment, shelter. They will never fail. The great government is behind it all, caring for him. We have something better yet. The King of heaven undertakes to take care of all who yield themselves fully to him. He says, "Take no thought for the morrow," "I will never leave nor forsake thee." And the resources and wisdom of the infinite are pledged to take care of us. Paul was so fully persuaded of it that he said, "I know whom I have believed and am persuaded that he is able to keep that which I have committed unto him, unto that day."

"When the billows would confound us,
Seek with foaming crest to drown us,
Tempests rage and war around us,
    God is with us still.

"He will never, never leave us,
Though all human hopes deceive us;
And though trusted friends may grieve us,
    God is with us still.

"For His mercy never faileth:
When the heart in anguish waileth,
Humble faith in Him availeth,
    God is with us still.

"Soon will come the dreadful hour
When we feel death's awful power;
Then our God shall be our tower.
    God is with us still.

"Let us then be always trusting,
On His blessed promise resting;
Knowing sure, whate'er the testing,
    God is with us still.

"Give thy all unto His keeping!
Cease thy doubts and sinful weeping!
His watch care is never sleeping.
    God is with us still."